HOW TO LIVE WELL, WHATEVER LIFE BRINGS

Love, Spiritual Growth, and Understanding Stress

❁

PILAR O. TAN, M.D.

ENDORSEMENTS

"This extensive work addresses an important issue for many today; that is coping with and growing through the difficulties, sufferings and disappointments of life. Your approach will provide very practical, effective ways for people to use when painful situations confront them as well as coping in a healthy way with everyday life. This is a subject well worth the effort to address as many struggle and suffer through life. The book has wonderful ideas and practical ways to empower people in need as well as simply living a healthy, full life. It has an important integration of good mental health practices, medical information and the wisdom of various faith traditions."

Sister Rosemary Moynihan, SC
General Superior
The Sisters of Charity of Saint Elizabeth
Convent Station, New Jersey

"Doctor Pilar Tan has written a very personal narrative with tenets that contain universal truths. She offers a well-constructed guide to having life-changing and/or life-affirming conversations with oneself. The roles that stress and emotions play in our daily activities are examined and their effects on health and quality of life are discussed in depth. The journey to being a "best" self is aided by checklists, anecdotal stories, organization referrals, and spiritual encouragements. It is not a work to be read through quickly. The questions raised in both secular and religious areas inspire contemplation and self-examination. Doctor Tan's son wished that a helpful and inspirational book be written. Edward's request has definitely been met."

Maureen Boyle
Independent Early Childhood Educator
Roselle, New Jersey

"This is a brilliant book. It is a devotional, a human development guide, an inspirational book and more rolled into one. One will have a hard time putting it down, also one that will often be referred to throughout one's life journey. I honestly think this book will become a bestseller. It is an incredible book with so many valuable facets in life and living that will benefit a whole lot of people. It is wonderful that you incorporated poems and prayers, and the humorous tidbits worked well too. I love your writing style. It is easy to understand, digest, and absorb. Anyone who reads it will be very blessed and grateful to have read it."

Emma Aliwalas, M.D.
Physical Medicine
Schenectady, New York

"This book is a story of a physician/mother who lost her beloved son Edward at the age of thirty-nine, and her effort at recovery from grief. The deep grief prompted the author, Dr. Pilar Tan, to harness her life experiences after years of caring for others to pull together her insights on how to move forward in life after tragic losses. Dr. Tan laid out 17 basic psychological concepts towards recovery from loss. The book should be useful reading for those who found themselves in similar situation."

Albert C. Gaw, M.D. DLFAPA
Clinical Professor of Psychiatry
UCSF, California

"This book is guided and inspired by the Holy Spirit. God used your son to encourage you...now you have the responsibility to share this valuable and inspirational book to many. A book that is filled with wisdom—knowledge from your experiences, family, friends, and most of all from the Holy Bible.

Conrad R. Zapanta, M.D.
Clinical Professor of Otolaryngology
Harrisonburg, Virginia

"It was pure serendipity that I had recently read *How to Live Well Whatever Life Brings* just before aspects of my own life became quite stressful. The insights of Dr. Pilar Tan come from a deep reservoir of wisdom gained from a lifetime of experiences—painful, joyful, and somewhere in between. Knowing that she herself has undergone so much and seen her way through made me receptive to her lessons. Her strong points come through to see these life experiences as gifts—what life GIVES us to help us reach our potential to become fully mature, resilient human beings. Take this opportunity to read this unique book by a physician-poet."

Ting Ting Larson Cheng
Writer-Editor
Roseville, Minnesota

"Dr. Pilar Tan's gentle spiritual nature shines through her insightful words which express the deepest yearning of the human heart, mind and soul in the pursuit of infinite love and infinite truth...which is God alone."

Sister Charitina Frabizio, M.A.,
Director of Religious Education
St. Anthony De Padua Parish,
Elizabeth, New Jersey

"This book is a powerful reflection of a woman's soul in the process of living; it touched my heart and stirred my soul. The love that is Pilar shines through the pages like the light of a new day. It is the love that makes her such a fine physician, parent and friend. This book is a triumph of the spirit."

Vincent A. Veneruso, M.A.
author of *Through My Eyes.*
Lakewood Ranch, Florida

"This book has helped me realize that I can spend some time meditating, praying, writing, and not feel guilty about taking time for myself."

Lois MacNamara, M.A.
Public school teacher,
Elizabeth, New Jersey

"This book is beautifully well-written...a learning experience...very touching...loving."

Lamberto A. Tan, M.D.,
Medical Director
Ocean Mental Health Services,
Bayville, New Jersey

"The book is filled with life experiences of the author, her attachment to her family particularly her son, growing up in the Philippines and her Christian values. I enjoyed her unique presentation and well-organized topics."

Jaime Q. Quintong
Financial Controller,
Edison, New Jersey

Copyright © 2014 Pilar O. Tan, M.D.

This text is a series of reflections, which include poetry and prose that express my knowledge as a physician about stress. It is not intended to diagnose, treat, or cure any condition. The reader is advised to seek assistance from a qualified health-care professional as necessary.

Copyright permission granted by:
Maha Milan
Yin and Yang picture
07890188650
www.sensiart.com

John Wiley & Sons, Inc.
Toward the Psychology of Being
Abraham Maslow

Books may be available at special quantity discounts for bulk purchases for sales promotions, premiums, fundraising, and educational use.
Books may be ordered through booksellers or by contacting:

Pilar O. Tan, M.D.
860 Park Avenue
Elizabeth, NJ 07208
908-403-6680

Visit us online at: www.pilartanmd.com

Because of the dynamic nature of the Internet, any web addresses or links contained in this book may have changed since publication and may no longer be valid.

Printed by Createspace.com

Certain stock imagery © Thinkstock

ISBN: 978-0-9909599-1-5 (paperback)
ISBN: 978-0-9909599-0-8 (hardcover)
ISBN: 978-0-9909599-2-2 (electronic)

Library of Congress Control Number: 2014919200

Understanding & Managing Stress
Journey to Holiness
Self-Development
Emotions
Mature Ego Defenses

This book is a tribute to my beloved son, Edward.

Proceeds will go to the humanitarian causes he dreamt of supporting.

Contents

PART TWO
STRESS

ACKNOWLEDGMENTS

ALMIGHTY GOD GAVE me the grace to do this monumental task of writing and the perseverance to complete this book. My gratitude goes to Dr. Lawrence Nardozzi whose loving support, friendship, and thought-provoking discussions were deeply appreciated.

Many people have supported me emotionally and spiritually; and others have helped in various ways as well: Dr. Claire Manfredi for editing this manuscript. Mrs. Ting Ting Larson Cheng for editing my poems. Mr. Vincent Veneruso for assisting me in the creation of this book. My daughter, Dr. Melin Tan-Geller; her husband, Dr. David Geller; and his mother, Mrs. Lea Geller; and sister, Atty. Suzette Geller. Sister Charitina Frabizio, especially for her prayers. My brother, Atty. Jose Mariano Tan; his wife, Dr. Neriza Tan; and their children, Atty. Jose Mario Tan and Dr. Jose Mariano Tan II. My sisters, Dr. Esperanza Elena Tan-Liong and Mrs. Josephine Palang. Justice Virginia Long, Dr. Florentina Teyu, Dr. Leda Sineneng, Ms. Jennie Macchiachera, Miss Jennifer Duran, Miss Johnna Dabu, Mr. Mario Cornacchia, Dr. Lamberto Tan, Mr. Arthur Lim, Ms. Maureen Boyle, Ms. Patricia Lynch, Sister Rosemary Moynihan, Mrs. Aida Gold, my classmates from the class of 1965 of UERM Medical Center, Philippines, Staci Kern, my Publishing Services Associate and Lynn David Newton, copy editor for Balboa Press.

This book would not exist without my son, Edward, in my life. He taught me how to write and he is my inspiration for writing this book.

My patients were instrumental in inspiring me to write about my medical knowledge on how to live well.

Thank you.

FOREWORD

W E LIVE IN an age of irony. With communication faster, easier, and cheaper than ever before, we have become in many ways much more isolated. While in the past, communication was often synonymous with interaction, today it has become an entity unto itself and does not necessarily imply or require personal contact, social cues, or humanistic nuances which have in the past defined so much of who we were, how we related to others, and in what ways we not only were perceived by others but how we were perceived by ourselves. What we lose in e-mail, text messages, Facebook, and Twitter is what has evolved over the millennia, namely facial cues, speech patterns, pitch changes, skin color, hand gestures, mannerisms, and the mind's amazing ability to process it all in a split second, granting insight into an individual's state of mind, emotion, and intentions. We lose human contact in its purest and simplest form—being literally next to someone. And with every lost interaction we lose emotional experience, opportunities with which to emotionally grow, test, err, succeed, and learn.

My mother, Dr. Pilar Tan, has produced a work that at its heart is rooted in her own personal journey and that reflects her emotional experiences over time. It has, at its center, the loving relationship and subsequent tragic loss of her son and my brother, Edward. However, it is colored by insight and advice garnered from a myriad of leaders spanning many ages and disciplines. It is, in its essence, an introspective glance into how emotional health, awareness, and maturity play pivotal roles in our day-to-day life. In doing so, my mother outlines a series of qualities or skill sets, which taken together allow for productivity, goal-oriented advancement, and balance, which have become harder to find in an increasingly complex world. Throughout the book, my mother weaves poetic verse, which she has herself written over many years, complementing each topic or focus in a deeply personal way and with a transparently humanistic touch.

The work is, in fact, a story, though it is not written as such. It tells an intimate tale of life, love, and loss. It is honest, simple, and forthcoming. It has relevance to nearly everyone in one way, shape, or form. It allows for a glimpse into a very real event, a deeply emotional personality, an introspective mind, and a spiritual being. It is work that would have made Edward very proud.

—Melin Tan-Geller, M.D.

INTRODUCTION

—————— ❈ ——————

A s long as we live, we encounter problems. If we continue to grow and overcome our problems successfully, we can become wiser by learning how to live well—adapting maturely to our lives each day.

Life is constantly changing. Nothing in life stays the same. Our sense of time is not constant. Days turn into months, months into years. Sometimes life moves sideways; often our lives move up or down. People who are afraid to live can live static lives, and their lives move sideways. People who really live fully go with the current of their lives. Sometimes they win in life, and their lives move upward; sometimes they lose, and their lives go downward.

In figure skating, you are taught to learn how to fall down before you are taught how to stand up correctly and skate. Life should be taught this way, too. We go to school to learn skills to have a productive life. We currently do not have a required school curriculum to handle life's setbacks. In 2013, President Obama allocated funds to promote wellness and resilience in schools in response to the Newtown, Connecticut, tragedy on December 14, 2012.

Most people learn through experience that in life we encounter painful difficulties: tragedies, illnesses, job and financial losses, failures, disasters, and accidents. Henry Wadsworth Longfellow wrote, "Into each life, some rain must fall." These are natural occurrences in life. When we are able to accept and anticipate these negative occurrences as normal in life, we spend less time asking, why me? We can deal with painful things when they come, and then spend less time thinking about our problems and more time focusing our energies on finding solutions. Life is not always what we want; it is what it is. And how we deal with our circumstances determines what our lives will become.

It is rare to live one's life without tragedy. A life without pain is a fantasy. Seneca wrote two millenniums ago, "Throughout our lifetime we have to learn how to live and how to die." We have to become emotionally mature to live well, to mourn our losses and move on. It is not what happens but rather what we do with what happens that determines the success of our life. William Arthur Ward wrote, "Greatness is not found in possession, power, position, or prestige. It is discovered in goodness, humility, service, and character." We spend a lot of time learning skills to earn a living and provide for our physical needs. We should also spend significant time learning how to fulfill our psychological needs (safety, belongingness, love, self-esteem, and self-realization), learning to know ourselves (individuation), and becoming our best.

In the eighteenth-century play *Nathan the Wise (Nathan der Weise)* by Gotthold Lessing, an angry sultan asked Nathan to identify the true religion—whether it was Christianity, Judaism, or Islam. Nathan, who was Jewish, told a story about an old man with three sons. The old man had a powerful, beautiful opal ring that possessed the great power of making the wearer become "loved of God and man." He wanted to give it to his sons as their inheritance, so he had two more identical rings made. After he died, the three sons went to a judge to ask him to identify the true ring. The judge explained that the power of the ring did not depend on the ring itself but on the work of each wearer or his ability to produce the results of what the ring had promised. The play illustrates our responsibility for our own life and its outcome. It is not outward circumstances, a specific religion, or what is given to us that will determine our life; it is what we do with ourselves and who we become.

William Earnest Henley made the same point in his poem "Invictus": "I am the master of my fate, the captain of my soul." Similarly, Shakespeare wrote in the play *Julius Caesar*, "The fault, dear Brutus, lies not in the stars, but in ourselves."

This book is about emotional maturity, mature ego defenses, managing stress, and more. It is about the five mature ego defenses, the journey to holiness, self-development, emotions, and managing stress in one's life. Emotional maturity means mental health and success in living. Mental health and physical health are fundamentally linked. Former US Surgeon General David Sacher, MD, PhD, tried to show this relationship when he said, "There is no health without mental health." Seventy-five percent of visits to doctors' offices concern stress-related ailment. Stress is linked to six leading causes of death: heart disease, cancer, lung ailments, accidents, cirrhosis of the liver, and suicide (APA, 2004). Older adults with serious long-term mental illnesses are at extremely high risk of a range of physical disorders, such as obesity, high blood pressure, diabetes, cardiovascular disease, pulmonary, and infectious diseases, which contribute to a lower lifespan by at least 10 percent. The National Institute of Mental Health (http://www.nami.org, 2013) reports that mental health disorders are experienced by an estimated 22 percent of American adults in a given year, nearly one in four. Untreated and mistreated mental illness cost the United States $105 billion in lost productivity each year, and US businesses foot up to $44 billion of this bill (BMJ, 1998; NMHA, 2001).

Emotional maturity and stress are inversely related. The more stress we have, the less emotionally mature we are prone to behave. We are prone to function maturely when we have less stress in our life. Because the amount and intensity of stress varies throughout our lifetime, our level of emotional maturity or mental health can reverse and change, depending on how we cope with the stress in our lives.

Americo was an emotionally mature forty-year-old, worked as an accountant, was happily married, and had a nine-year-old son; but by the time I saw him at forty-three years old, he was jobless, had been drinking heavily for a year, and had moved back to his parents' house because he was unable to support himself. His wife and son had died in an accident over a year before this. I referred him to a psychiatrist, a social worker, Alcoholics

Anonymous, and a Bible study group that met twice a week. He was able to stop drinking; his psychiatrist stopped his psychotropic medications after six months; and he recently found another accounting job. His coping skills for his losses were not mature, but he was able to *become* mature—able to love, work, play, and be effective in solving his day-to-day problems after a year of treatment and hard work. He told me, "I learned that you have to live through the pain. You cannot bury it with alcohol."

Emotional maturity affects how we think, feel, and act as we cope with life. It determines our ability to make choices, relate to others, and manage our problems. Emotional maturity helps us avoid unhealthy habits and influences our health choices positively, thereby giving us a chance to enjoy a healthy lifestyle. We have a great chance of staying physically healthy when we are emotionally mature.

Our emotional maturity determines our morality, for it is not the laws of the countries nor the superego that make us do virtuous things. And it is not the rules of various religions that determine how good we are; it is our love for God, self-love, and love for others. We usually start to learn and develop emotional maturity as we grow into our early school years or early teens. In my experience, some children are taught to share and give as early as six years old. Their parents believe that children who learn to give early in life (altruism—love) are happier and do not become spoiled and selfish. Parents show love by being affectionate and by giving them hugs and praises for their good behavior. When parents have a good sense of humor, their children learn to see the funny side of life early in their lives (humor). Discipline is also taught starting when they are toddlers. Children develop good behavior, and when they start school, they do their homework before they play or watch television (suppression—self-discipline). Some parents are good about explaining to their children the consequences of their behavior and the anticipated consequences for their choices (anticipation). Parents also show their children different ways of expressing their uncomfortable feelings, such as disappointments, by letting them draw pictures or build new toys (sublimation—creativity). So some people mature early; others never grow up. However, developing emotional maturity can be a lifelong process. Like love, emotional maturity has many components. We can be mature in some of our reasoning and behavior at work but immature in handling our intimate relationships. Fully developed emotional maturity is not ordinary. How many people do you know who are fully mature emotionally?

To complement this text, I have included my own poems. Some I composed while writing this book; others I wrote a few years back, while my son, Edward, was around to edit and teach me. I wrote vignettes from composite stories of patients. (Identifying information was altered to ensure confidentiality.)

In the gospel of Matthew, Jesus said, 'What, then, will a person gain if that person wins the whole world and ruins his (or her) life?' (Matthew 16:26, *Jerusalem Bible*) When we live deliberately, we know what we are doing is right or wrong. Knowing right from wrong may make us do the right thing and protect us from harming anyone. When we are doing something wrong, we usually do not want to tell the truth about what we are doing. Our wrongdoings escalate when we cover up our initial mistake. One small lie can lead to bigger and bigger lies. One small mistake can escalate into bigger and bigger mistakes that can cause greater damage.

People who are unaware of their motivation or who ignore it may commit wrong, even evil deeds. However, sometimes we are awakened by the pain from our wrong deeds and become better persons. Carl Jung wrote, "There is no coming to consciousness without pain." On a similar note, Benjamin Franklin wrote, "Those things that hurt, instruct."

Moses received the Ten Commandments on Mt. Sinai. We can reflect on them daily and correct ourselves when we deviate from these rules. I believe that these commandments are God's gift to us. They can protect us from harming ourselves and others.

The message of the Ten Commandments is to love. The Ten Commandments can be easily remembered and practiced by loving ourselves and loving others. The most practical way of loving God is to love everybody unconditionally; that is, to be a good human being. It is challenging to love this way. In my experience, this is not usually done, and it is difficult to do; but it is good to love unconditionally because doing so brings peace, energy, and so much joy. Unconditional love can make the people we love grow.

In a world filled with corruption and poverty, a world that values power and material things more than anything else, we can still rise above the crowd and live a virtuous life. We are not only physical beings; we are spiritual beings having a physical existence. All of us have a divine part in us; God is within us. When we love ourselves as well as others, we love God. A wise friend told me, "Treat everybody with love, and you will have no problems with people." I told him, "You are enlightened, my friend. I know that life is very difficult, the human condition is very difficult, and to love everybody is very difficult." He answered, "Who told you that to love is easy?"

It is my hope that through reading this book, you will learn and implement the seventeen skill sets for living well, thereby developing emotional maturity, and managing stress. You will live with love in your heart; you will live a balanced life of love, work, and play and be effective in solving your day-to-day problems. You will have health, inner peace, more happiness, joy, energy, and the motivation to make your life better no matter what life brings, and you will make this world a better place. It will fulfill my deceased son's wish to write something that would make a difference in people's lives. After he got married, he was so busy with his law career, bike racing, fundraising for the Leukemia and Lymphoma Society, interviewing freshman applicants for Georgetown University, and doing carpentry work that he was unable to make the time to write a "helpful and inspirational book" before he died. I am carrying on his dream as a tribute to him.

Justice Virginia Long of the New Jersey Supreme Court delivered this speech at the Middlesex County Bar Association Memorial Service on October 30, 2008.

Edward Dylan Tan died on July 30, 2008, at the age of 39. Although he only danced on this earth a short time, he accomplished much as a lawyer: first as a clerk for the New Jersey Supreme Court, then as a Deputy Attorney General, and finally as a private practitioner at Bressler, Amery & Ross. He was a brilliant and accomplished lawyer, a tactical thinker who in law, as in life, was always a step ahead. But that says much too little. Edward was a quintessential Renaissance man. He knew something about everything and a lot about many things. He was engaged with the world. He read voraciously—fiction, non-fiction—poetry and prose—Eastern and Western—and a section of my library at home is devoted to the poetry books he gave me—introducing me to Italian, Hungarian, French, and Asian writers I have come to love. He was a writer. He wrote spare, elegant prose and imaginative, mellifluous, meditative poetry. He was a master woodworker who did all of his own cabinetry. He baked pies and brought them to our house on Thanksgiving. He raced bikes—soaring nationally and internationally, and used that skill to raise prodigious amount of money for charity. He was an animist who saw the soul in all of nature's creations, especially his own dogs, who still look for him today. He was a great laugher—sending his friends slyly hysterical cartoons. He was a great friend, a great son, and a great husband to his wife Kimberley who is here with us today.

Although we miss him, gone too soon, we obtain solace because we see Edward today on the terms coined by the poet and flyer John Gillespie Magee—For us he has merely slipped the surly bonds of earth and to us he is free—'Dancing in the skies on laughter-silvered wings, sunward climbing, joining the tumbled mirth of sun-split clouds' and 'doing a hundred things we have never dreamed of.'

Godspeed, Edward.

Here is Dr. Melin Tan-Geller's tribute to Edward:

"I'd like to begin by thanking everyone for being here and for the incredible support that our family has received during the past few days.

I knew Edward Dylan Tan all my life; having said that, my life and our family's life were so enriched by his presence and by his brilliance. My brother was an amazing person. He was quiet, composed, thoughtful, sincere and respectful. For those of you who were present at my wedding, you will recall the memorable speech that he gave in which he talked about picking and choosing your family. While I would agree that you cannot pick and choose who your family members are, if the choice were mine to make, I would have chosen him.

Beneath an unassuming exterior, lay a depth of insight and knowledge. He was accomplished in his own right, having graduated from Georgetown and gone on to receive his law degree from the University of San Diego. He had the honor of clerking for our dear friend Justice Virginia Long in the New Jersey Supreme Court and then became a Deputy Attorney General for the State of New Jersey. Most recently, he worked as an associate for Bressler, Amery, and Ross.

Beyond Ed's professional accomplishments, his most defining characteristic was his extraordinary literary talent. He had a true love of literature and he was the most well-read person that I have ever known. This permeated his everyday life. Every word he spoke had meaning and purpose. He was an artist of words.

I came across a paper that he wrote way back in college, about heroism in John Milton's well-known work, *Paradise Lost,* which I'd like to share today. The paper's subtitle was "One must think like a hero in order to be a merely decent human being." In this, he wrote: "Despite an inadequate knowledge of the future, a hero decides on the most favorable course of action and then makes every effort to strive for the best possible outcome. The heroic process does not depend on the success or failure of the endeavor, but rather on the individuals' willingness to propel themselves in the face of all disenchantment, to move beyond known boundaries and ascend toward greater levels of self-actualization. The aim ultimately lies in the enhancement of others. Thus, a hero acts in the face of infinite odds, acting not with certainty, but with a faith in individual judgment...."

This heroism that Ed described in Milton's writing is reflective of how he lived his life, how he interacted with other people, and how he conducted himself. Since childhood, my brother has been my hero. I am sure that there are others today for whom he was also a hero. Regardless, I have no doubt that we will all remember him as a decent human being and so much more.

Thank you."

Here is one of Edward's essays published in Calliope, a literary magazine of the Pingry School, in December 1986 when he was in twelfth grade.

Castles in the Sand

The sand appeared almost white beneath the silent sky, yet he did not turn his eyes away, preferring the vision of the city which rose before him. Waves of heat had given the illusion of unseen flames, burning through streets and upon the dry ground below, buildings and towers seemingly alive in the brilliance of the light. Mesmerized by the movement upon movement of the clouds and their myriad shadows flowing across the city, his heart beat slowly, surrendered to the fervor of the landscape. A listless hand passed above his brow, and the image was within his thoughts as an unforgettable fire.

She watched him with pleasant concern amid her book and his sleep, the still figure of the child upon the sand and the sun and the waves, bringing her to a smile as she turned away from the page. It was a perfect day.

"He always did enjoy the shore."

"Like his Mom."

She kissed the reclining figure beside her and closed her eyes to the heat of the sun and the sound of the waves. Still, she could not displace the burning of the sand beneath her; the sensation so intense as if out of a memory between agony and pleasure.

She called to him. The afternoon grew darker into night. He stared for the moment at the wind in the dry sand stirring its particles of people through the city no longer gold but only so much darkness. Her hand embraced his. They turned and walked in the final light. She sat with the child in her arms, staring at the night sky. As the child lay asleep, she listened to the wind exchanging secrets with the dry grass. In her hand she held some flowers the child had collected during the day. They had been walking in the hills and had found a place to rest among some rocks. The child pointed to a group of beautiful flowers growing between the crevices. The child asked how long the flowers would live, and when she said the winter frost would kill them, the child uprooted the flowers to save them. She wished it were so easy to save the child as she held the flowers.

She was not sure why she should remember the city as it lay half-diminished in the August tide ebb.

PART ONE
MATURE EGO DEFENSES
AND BEYOND

Optimize our ability to have rich and good relationships, job satisfaction, better overall health, and fulfillment in life.

CHAPTER 1

―――――― ❖ ――――――

Mature Ego Defenses

Adaptation to life means continued growth.
—George E. Vaillant, MD

HERE ARE SEVENTEEN skill sets you can learn and develop to live well whatever life brings. These include the five *Mature ego defenses*: altruism (love), suppression (self-discipline), anticipation, sublimation (creativity), and humor;(5), faith in God, acceptance of suffering, peace and joy; (3) self-love and self-esteem, courage, hope, work, understanding, play, happiness;(7) energy; (1)and handling stress.(1) (See Appendix A.)

Learning and implementing these seventeen skill sets allows us to master our fate and life better. We can be our best and make the best of our situation no matter what life brings. We can continuously grow and live in a state of becoming as long as we strive to be our best. We are not better or worse than another person; what matters is we are the best that we can become.

A rose is the best when it grows to become the best rose, not an orchid. Be true to your best self; do not try to become somebody else. Time is limited. Spend your time on what is most important to you. Find and live your own meaning in life, and do not wish to have someone else's life. Each one of us has our individual purpose and trials. Live what is true, good, and beautiful in yourself. You need to keep living and learning to enrich your life. It takes effort and courage to live by trial and error, to find fulfillment in yourselves and others.

We can use our minds, hearts, and souls to know and understand our emotions. We have the free will to choose and decide what to do with ourselves and our lives. We also have the ability to be aware of ourselves. Being self-aware, we can correct or change ourselves. This is one of our God-given gifts. Some people believe that other animals do not have this attribute.

For example, when a peahen was lost for days at the Bronx Zoo and a newscaster commented that these peahens were allowed to come and go from their shelters at any time, the lost peahen did not go back on her own. It appears lower animals do not possess the free will that human beings possess. When we are confronted with a given situation, we can learn to choose thoughts and feelings that lead to constructive behaviors for ourselves and others. We can be proactive instead of reactive. We can choose what to think, what to feel, and what to do should a certain situation develop. These thoughts, feelings, and behaviors that you can develop are synergistic and interrelated skills for you to practice and build upon throughout life.

You can learn these seventeen skill sets—which include the mature ego defenses—growing up at home; in schools; in places of worship; from families and friends; by reading or listening to tapes; through educational media, retreats, meditation, or self-reflection; and by dream analysis.

Once you learn these qualities, some become a habit in a short time. With others, you must remind yourselves throughout your lifetime to implement them. They require your will, courage, effort, determination, perseverance, and persistence. It is good to practice and apply all of them daily as a way of life.

The book *Adaptation to Life*, by Harvard psychiatrist Dr. George E. Vaillant, is a research study about the development of Harvard male college students. Vaillant followed their lives for thirty-five years and interpreted their behaviors using the ego defenses that Sigmund Freud and his daughter, Anna Freud dedicated their lives' work to.

Ego defenses can be mature, neurotic, immature, or psychotic. People use mature ego defenses from ages twelve and onward. Again, *mature ego defenses* are suppression (self-discipline), sublimation (creativity), anticipation, humor, and altruism (love). (See Appendix A.) These are skills we develop within ourselves. They are distinct from intelligence quotient (IQ), physical maturation, and cognitive, intellectual, or psychosocial development. In the Vaillant study, the evolution of mature defenses seemed independent of social or genetic predisposition. The ego matured in adverse conditions as well as in privileged circumstances.

Ego defenses are dynamic and reversible. Immature defenses can become mature, and mature defenses can change to immature ones, depending on how much stress a person is experiencing. We tend to use immature, neurotic, or even psychotic defenses when we are under severe stress, even if we have previously shown mature ego defenses under normal circumstances. Our brain does not function well under severe stress. We lose our cognitive ability under severe stress.

When my son Edward was sick, developed uncontrolled diabetes mellitus, was hospitalized, and subsequently committed suicide, my whole mind and body felt numbed and paralyzed. What is even more tragic is the fact that what happened to my son was not his fault. I just cannot explain the details. I just have to accept that he is dead and there is nothing I can do to change that.

I was in shock and was emotionally numbed. I suffered from acute stress disorder for three or four weeks. I purposely avoided doing things that required personal decision-making. Through time, prayers, discipline, reading inspirational literature, writing poetry, being with nature and beauty, listening to music, taking good care of myself, taking good care of my patients, minimizing my other stresses, lots of emotional support from family and friends, courage, and effort, I recovered. During the following months, I focused on the work I was doing by consciously applying suppression (self-discipline). Using all my energy to do my work with extreme self-discipline made me feel so tired afterward. I understood and mastered the ego defenses while studying four years of psychiatry in medical school, but it was only during this very difficult time that I used my will to consciously implement the mature ego defenses daily as my coping skills.

According to Vaillant, ego defenses are unconscious coping skills that we all use. Defenses are mental processes that our egos use to resolve conflicts among the four guiding lights of our inner life: our conscience, reality, important people, and instinct. However, ego defenses can be used consciously, by choice, through discipline and self-reflection. I have experienced doing this successfully. I would think of how to respond and consciously use mature ego defenses. For example, I was in between seeing patients when I remembered something about Edward. Instead of dwelling on it, I consciously chose not to think about it. I used suppression (self-discipline), and reviewed my next set of patients' medical records. I finished my work before I resumed my thoughts about Edward.

A patient brought her mother from another country and asked me to check her. She had no appointment and no insurance. I examined her and did not charge her. I consciously used altruism (love). I heard a piano piece on the radio that instantly reminded me of Edward, because it was one of his favorite pieces of music. Instead of feeling very sad, I wrote a poem about it. I chose sublimation (creativity) as my ego defense. One time, I forgot my umbrella at the hospital. Instead of being upset, I consciously used humor. I told my sister, "At least I did not forget our sandwiches for lunch," and we laughed. I had a very busy day at work and kept on working to finish my schedule. I comforted myself by planning that after my office hours I would walk to the park with my friend and would have a relaxing and fun time. I used anticipation. My experiences made me think that if I can write about these mature ego defenses and help people learn to use them consciously to handle their day-to-day problems, then this book will be a worthwhile effort.

Emotional maturity equates to health, which is success in living. People who are emotionally mature are usually physically and mentally healthy. They are more self-disciplined and do not usually indulge in unhealthy habits such as smoking, alcohol abuse, and overeating. Physical and emotional health can correlate with mature ego defenses. It is distinct from luck, fame, or material success. Our ability to acquire and use mature ego defenses depends on:

- Our upbringing: When we grow up with parents who taught us love, self-discipline, and responsibility, we have a good chance of becoming emotionally mature.
- The amount of stress we undergo: If our stresses are enormous—if, for example, we constantly live with chaos—we may use less mature ego defenses or less adaptive defenses. When we live in a loving and nurturing environment, we have the occasion to use mature ego defenses.
- The strength of our ego (our conscious self): When we are strong emotionally, we can handle stress well and, in turn, use mature ego defenses to cope with and solve our problems. *Ego* means the conscious aspect of our mind that develops through contact with the external world. It is the thinking, feeling, and acting self that is aware of itself and the environment. People who have strong self-love and self-esteem may handle stress well compared to those deficient in self-love and self-esteem. Strong faith in God, regardless of the religion we practice, also gives us ego strength. In general, given the same circumstances, stage IV spiritual people (purposeful powerful.wordpress.com)

handle stressful situations better than agnostics or atheists. Spiritual people tend to worry less and are able to let go and live in the present.

• The length of time we are in a destructive environment and the number of destructive people in our lives: The loss of one good relationship is not as devastating as having a continuous interaction with destructive people.

• The presence of mature, healthy, intimate and loving relationships in our lives: These would include psychotherapy, Bible studies, support groups such as AA, and prayer groups. Intimacy makes us grow. Love heals.

• The will to grow: We can mature if we choose to work hard to become mature.

• God's grace: I encountered people in my forty years of practicing medicine as an internist who were immature and even disorganized in their lives. Without any impetus that was obvious to me, I saw them become good and loving individuals. I believe that life continually holds the possibility of change for the better. To me, that possibility is the freely given love and favor of God. As the saying goes, God acts in mysterious ways.

If you did not learn and acquire these mature ego defenses while growing up, or if you are not consistently using them because of the enormous amount of stress you are having, you can learn, actively remember, and consciously implement them at any time. You can take the time to reflect on your life's problems and patiently practice using these five mature ego defenses consciously so that you are able to love, work, and play.

In his book *The Power of Maturity*, Rabbi Louis Binstock enumerates ten pillars of maturity which are outcomes of using the five mature ego defenses. Dr. Will Menninger, founder of the Menninger Clinic, similarly suggests seven criteria for emotional maturity. Using the five mature ego defenses results in greater acceptance of your own reality and identity, flexible adaptation to change, resistance to stress, and an ability to love, work, and play.

ALTRUISM (LOVE)

> "Whatever is your problem, love is the answer."
> —A common proverb

The word *love* is one of the most common words we use, and it can mean many, many things. The Greeks use the words *agape* (altruism), *philia* (friendship) and *eros* (romantic love).

One of the best definitions of love is *altruism*, which is one of our mature ego defense mechanisms. Altruism is about giving and forgiving. When we experience loss, there are so many things that we think we could have done differently. And there are some people that have caused us pain, so it is important to forgive. When we forgive ourselves and others, we give ourselves the best gift we can give ourselves. We will not be able to move on with our lives peacefully, joyfully, and with acceptance if we do not forgive.

Martha is angry at her former son-in-law since her daughter died. It is now fifteen years since her daughter's death, and she is chronically depressed, has become an alcoholic, and still carries a lot of resentment toward her son-in-law. She told me, "I can never forgive the way he treated me after my daughter died. I am always thinking of how he had ruined and is ruining my life." We have to take responsibility for our responses. We need to learn to be proactive instead of being reactive.

Forgive
Be like the sun
That shines underneath
The cloudy sky.

Be like a hero
That forgets, forgives,
Our imperfect world.
Be like your favorite pet dog
who does not carry grudges.

Make a habit
To start each day anew.

Altruism is also about doing something or sacrificing for the sake of others. People from the Philippines (my country of origin) as well as those who live surrounded by poverty while growing up, like those from other third world countries, learn the virtue of altruism early in life. It is a custom to share what we have with others who are less fortunate. While growing up in the Philippines, I witnessed my family and neighbors giving to others who were less fortunate. It was a way of life.

The more resources we have, the more we give to others. I was conversing with people from Cuba who told me that it was also one of their customs to help their family and friends. Altruism is a behavior practiced all over the world, especially here in America. There are so many wealthy Americans and people who give so much to the community and to organizations. Albert Einstein wrote, "Only a life lived for others is a life worthwhile."

The first letter of St. Paul to the Corinthians is another description of love:

If I speak in human and angelic tongues, but do not have love, I am a resounding gong or a clashing cymbal. And if I have the gift of the prophecy, and comprehend all mysteries and all knowledge; if I have all faith so as to move mountains, but do not have love, I am nothing. If I give away everything I own, and if I hand my body over so that I may boast, but do not have love, I gain nothing.

Love is patient, love is kind. It is not jealous, [love] is not pompous, it is not inflated, it is not rude, it does not seek its own interests, it is not quick-tempered, it does not brood over injury, it does not rejoice over wrongdoing but rejoices with the truth. It bears all things, believes all things, hopes all things, endures all things.

Love never fails. If there are prophecies, they will be brought to nothing; if tongues, they will cease; if knowledge, it will be brought to nothing. For we know partially and we prophesy partially, but when the perfect comes, the partial will pass away. When I was a child, I used to talk as a child, think as a child, reason as a child; when I became a man, I put aside childish things. At present we see indistinctly, as in a mirror, but then face to face. At present I know partially; then I shall know fully as I am fully known. So faith, hope, love remain, these three; but the greatest of these is love. (1 Corinthians 13:1–13)

Living is about loving.

To summarize:

- Love is patient. We do not become angry easily. We make allowances for people's faults and insults.
- Love is kind. We return good for evil. We give regardless of whether the person deserves it.
- Love is courteous. We are polite.
- Love is unselfish. We are more concerned about giving than receiving.
- Love is guileless. We do not do evil or harmful things to people.
- Love is forgiving. We forget the wrong things that people do to us. We erase them from our hearts and minds.
- Love is humble. We are not arrogant and rude. We ask for forgiveness when we hurt someone.
- Love is sincere. Love rejoices in the truth. It seeks a sincere acceptance of the truth.
- Love is hopeful. We are encouraged to do better. There is hope for brighter things.

- Love is considerate.
- Love is understanding.
- Love is unconditional. We love everybody. We separate the person from the behavior. We can dislike the behavior but love the person.
- Love is forever. Love never ends. It endures.

Loving by doing some of the things described as love is not so difficult, but to love doing all the things as described by St. Paul to the Corinthians or as Christ's life demonstrated is very difficult. It requires a lifelong conscious will and work to achieve.

I memorized St. Paul's descriptions of love and meditate on them often. St. Paul's writing is a good reminder to read or recall daily. I have a plaque containing passages from this letter to the Corinthians in front of my desk and I read it when something bothers me.

The best gift we can give to ourselves as well as to others is our love. Real love is always constructive. Those who are certain of our love generally value our advice. Parents who love their children are usually successful in guiding them.

Love includes friendship (*philia*), and friendship expresses love. Ella Wheeler Wilcox wrote, "All love that has not friendship for its base is like a mansion built upon the sand." Friendship means helping each other, having fun together, sharing the good and bad times, and having open communication; it is life-enriching, and there is peace in the relationship. Friends make time to discuss disagreements and share thoughts and feelings about the issues that are in conflict. True friends are loyal to one another and do not intentionally hurt each other. I am confident that my friends will never do anything intentionally to hurt me and vice versa. When we need support, we can count on them for help. We establish friendships throughout our lifetime. Friendship requires skill. The longer friendships last, the better the quality of those friendships becomes.

Love is empathetic. It possesses the ability to feel what another person is feeling. It enables us to experience another person's emotions as our own. I have read a commentary about our handling of the Vietnam War that said many people believe that we lacked empathy for the Vietnamese at that time.

Where does love come from? I believe love comes from God. Love is one of life's mysteries.

Unconditional Love (One)
Loving ourselves,
everybody,
like appreciating
the glitter
of every star
in the sky.

Creating ourselves, recreating ourselves;
creating our responses,
pliable as a piece of gum.

Planting our landscapes,
vast and varied
as the seashells;
bright and beautiful
as tulips in springtime.

Accepting the pain,
the rain as rainbows
and spices.
Accepting the selves,
varied as flowers
in May.
Accepting the selves,
the colors as they are.

Loving without conditions,
loving without demands;
we give and forgive

unconditionally
to ourselves, family,
friends, patients
and to the world.

Edward gave this to me one Mother's Day.
(It is a 1915 song composed by Theodore F. Morse, lyrics
by Howard Johnson.)

M-O-T-H-E-R
"M" is for the million things she gave me,
"O" means only that she's growing old,
"T" is for the tears she shed to save me,
"H" is for her heart of purest gold;
"E" is for her eyes, with love-light shining.
"R" means right, and right she'll always be,
Put them all together, they spell "MOTHER,"
A word that means the world for me.

REQUISITES OF CONSTRUCTIVE ROMANTIC LOVE (*EROS*)

Romantic love is a unique form of love and has other requisites besides unconditional love and *philia* (friendship).

To grow in romantic love, we first have to have a formed identity. We must know ourselves and be able to describe and share who and what we are, what we want for our life, what values we cannot compromise, and what values are negotiable. You cannot love yourselves and be true to yourselves if you do not know who you are. You cannot share yourselves with others if you do not know yourselves.

Romantic love involves respect. It is valuing another person for who and what that person is. You may not like some characteristics of that person, but you esteem that individual's uniqueness. You value the person's individuality, autonomy, separateness, and independence.

John likes to play golf. His girlfriend respected his time to play golf without her. She supports the hobbies that John has even when she herself has no interest in joining. In mature romantic love, we can each independently fulfill our emotional needs and not become jealous of our partner's other relationships.

Romantic love requires work. It takes time and energy to love. When you are helping somebody or you are communicating, you use your energy. As when tending your garden, you spend time taking care of, being with, learning about, and teaching that other person. You are motivated to give of yourselves freely. You are not manipulative. You do not give in order to get something back. You give because it makes you happy to give.

Romantic love requires courage. You need to get rid of your fears in order to love—to share who you are, to confront another person, when necessary, with the things he or she is doing. You have to take a risk to love. Love can hurt you deeply. The person you love can leave you.

Romantic love requires discipline. Even when you feel like yelling at your partner, you can restrain yourselves from doing so. You can hold your angry feelings for the right time to express them.

Maria was upset when her boyfriend showed up two hours late without calling her. She did not show her anger and calmly went with him to the wedding they planned to attend. Only when they came back from the affair did she confront her boyfriend about it.

Romantic love requires judgment. It requires deliberate analysis of the situation. Couples have to make sure that they are compatible and their lives can blend together harmoniously. You have to know yourselves well and the other person well, also to know that you are involved with the right person, and you must be the right person for each other.

It is good to think about the future. Do you think you are both responsible and emotionally mature enough to be together harmoniously into your old age?

Joyce met her boyfriend while attending college. They were raised in different cultures. She is an immigrant from Chile. Her boyfriend was born here, and his parents' family lived in the US for five generations. They have irreconcilable differences, and both decided to end their relationship after six months.

The dating stage is a good time to get to know one another. It is good to avoid getting physically involved. Instead, become good friends first. There is a hormone, oxytocin, that is released when you are physically involved and that makes you become attached to the person with whom you are in love. Oxytocin is secreted in both men and women. You suffer more when you break up a relationship that involved sexual attachment.

I know some successful romantic love relationships that happened because both partners used good judgment in looking at their situations realistically. They were also lucky to meet and find the right person.

Romantic love requires communication. You have to take the time to share your thoughts and feelings, to share what goes on with your lives. You need to learn how to listen to what your partner is sharing, to approve and appreciate the other person's unique self.

Julia and Dante schedule one afternoon a week just to share and discuss things that are happening with themselves, their work, their relatives, and other relationships.

Romantic love requires a will and a commitment to grow. You commit yourselves to have an exclusively steady boyfriend or girlfriend. You spend time to see if you become fonder of each other, whether you like each other and get along well as time goes by. Sometimes you may not have loving feelings, but you can will to be loving. You can choose to love even when you do not have the feelings of love.

Romantic love is a phrase that is commonly used to mean sexual love. It is a feeling of falling in love and being in love. It seems to be involuntary, not a conscious choice; it just seems to happen. However, this ecstatic feeling may not last forever. Sooner or later you may fall out of love if that love does not develop in other ways. It is important to realize this, because you can misinterpret this experience. You can think that something is wrong with your relationship when your romantic feelings fade or disappear. Although it is a good thing to experience the feelings of romantic love, and it can be a beautiful occurrence, real love as described by St. Paul and friendship are the important ingredients for a happy and successful relationship.

In real romantic love, you experience admiration, respect, and physical chemistry, which are good foundations for married or committed relationships. *Physical chemistry* is the comfortable feeling of just being together. *Admiration* is appreciation of the qualities that another person has. You can be attracted by your similarities, but you grow from your complementary differences. In harmonious relationships, you function together as a team. You let the person who happens to be good at the task needed to be solved do the work.

David is good at negotiating, and when his girlfriend needed to buy a car, she asked him to go with her.

Romantic Love—
How I Love You
I love you,
day and night,
until the breeze of feelings
become unconscious.

I feel joy and gratitude
as I sit by the ocean
having happy thoughts
and energy to grow.

I wish you happiness
anywhere you are,
anytime, all the time;

while you are in the green mountains
that are forever green
where love stayed forever alive
in your heart.

Unhealthy experiences of romantic love (*eros*)

Dependency

A common behavior, wrongly labeled as love, is *dependency*.
Dependent people want to be loved. Their energies are focused on
trying to be the person they think their partner wants, rather than
sharing who they truly are. Because another person can never
give them what they ought to provide for themselves, they are
angry at that person and blame him or her for their misery. Some
people purposely give to somebody because they are interested
in getting something back. Dependent people rely on others for
their emotional needs. They love because they want to be loved.
They are more concerned about what other people can give them
instead of giving or loving others unconditionally.

When we are emotionally dependent, we lack intimacy in
our communication. When we are not intimate, our relationship
will not grow. Dependent people cannot stand on their own two
feet. As soon as they break up one relationship, they find another
person to fall in love with right away.

I asked a patient two months after her divorce how she was
doing and she said, "I am doing fine and I am happy. I am
planning to move in with my new boyfriend." She was dependent
and went from a bad situation to perhaps another one.

If you happen to be dependent, work on becoming responsible
for your life—for your physical and emotional needs—before
getting involved in a romantic relationship. You may need to heal
your "child within," grieve your losses, be true to who you really

are, and fulfill your own physical and psychological needs before spending your time and energy finding a romantic relationship.

> **Dependent Love**
> It was never
> dark all the time,
> but my emotional need
> blinded me
> and prevented me
> from seeing.
>
> It was not my soul
> that needed cleansing.
> It was my emotional need
> that wanted the relationship
> to go on.
>
> It was not outward circumstances
> that caused my pain.
> It was my demand
> and need that made me
> destructive to myself.

INFATUATION

Infatuation is a temporary strong sexual attraction for another person. The play *Phantom of the Opera* is built around a classic example. The infatuated one often does not know the other person very well but is just physically attracted and longs to be with that one all the time. Sexual desire can be aroused by instinct, infatuation, excitement, projection, anger, or the desire to control, destroy, or punish. I heard a story about a couple who feel strong sexual passion when they are angry at each other. Infatuation is like being very much in love, but it is not real love. You do not exercise your will and judgment in choosing the person that you are infatuated with.

Healthy relationships

Agape, philia, eros

Altruism, friendship and romantic love are components of healthy relationships that can lead to successful relationships. Poet Rainer Marie Rilke wrote, "For one human being to love another: that is perhaps the most difficult task of all ... the work for which all other work is but a preparation. It is a high inducement to the individual to ripen ... a great exacting claim upon us, something that chooses us out and calls us to vast things." Pierre Teilhard De Chardin, SJ, wrote, "Love alone is capable of uniting living beings in such a way as to fulfill and complete them, for it alone takes them and joins them by what is deepest in themselves."

Marriage

Marriage is the most complex of human love relationships. If our relationship is leading to marriage, certain topics need to be discussed, such as having children, flexibility, unity, respect for individual differences, conflict negotiation, trust, creativity, commitment, and cooperation. Most importantly, work on effective intimate communication. You need to practice humility to reveal your true selves, your "shadows." Do this before or during the engagement period. I believe it is a good sign if you enjoy talking with each other about anything and everything that is mutually important. It is also a good sign when you enjoy or are comfortable being together even without doing any activities. Business management skills are also required in marriage.

Marriage requires serious thinking and decision making. You can change your career with fewer problems than when ending a marriage. My marriage ended after twelve years. However, my parents had a real and a great marriage. They solved their problems together and happily lived throughout the ups and downs of their lives together. They were committed to love each other and stay together until death. My mother took good care of my father until his last breath.

Edward wrote the essay quoted below while at Pingry High School. (He attended the Pingry School from second to twelfth grade.) He read great world literature and wrote extensively while at Pingry and during his undergraduate time at Georgetown University.

Death remains inevitable, but we may live in our time if we give ourselves to love. The immovable walls surround the length of our existence, but we may remove them for maybe there are miracles, but not enough people to believe. And perhaps we may live our dreams, if we have faith in our souls to love and be loved.

What separates life from existence, the soul from the machine, is love. As children, the ability to open our passions was natural. Growing up introduced rationality; we are sent away to be taught how to be sensible, practical, logical. However, love is not rational, it just is. The truth we must find is the love within us. Society, "distracted from distraction by distraction," forsakes people.

Suppression (self-discipline)

To solve your problems, you need to discipline yourselves and to learn to delay your gratification. You can choose how to respond to what you think, what you feel, or what you do at any given moment. You can concentrate on one thing and think about your other tasks later on. In psychiatry, this ego defense is called *suppression*. If you need to do something important at the present, you can think of other things later.

When we suffer a loss, we cannot spend our time thinking only about our loss. We have to continue to work, to love, and to play as well. We have to continue living. We need to concentrate on what we have to do in the present. We can tell ourselves, "I will think about these other things tomorrow." This requires self-discipline.

During my grieving and bereavement process I made sure that I functioned well at work and disciplined myself to concentrate on taking care of my patients. I also disciplined myself to stay healthy. I ate healthy foods, slept eight hours a day, and did at least twenty minutes of aerobic exercises each day. Sometimes I did not feel like exercising, but I disciplined myself to do it. I also did arts and crafts, prayed, read inspirational books, wrote poetry, and played the piano to relax and comfort myself. I made my health a priority in my day-to-day schedule.

Self-discipline is necessary also in controlling your mind and emotions, and in changing yourselves. You can stop eating sweets and gradually learn to eat more healthy foods, even if you do not like them, by using your mind. You can successfully stop smoking, do physical exercise, or do whatever you decide to do that is good for you through self-discipline. One helpful way of implementing self-discipline or self-mastery is to associate the constructive things you need to be doing with good feelings while doing them. When you meditate, you can activate the alpha and delta brain waves, which help your memory and also relax you. These are helpful ways of implementing self-discipline.

Self-discipline is necessary in controlling your emotions, especially your anger. Take time to think and understand. Untamed feelings of anger can cause destructive behaviors.

Dina spanked her son because he said something that made her very angry. They fought, and then her son ran away from home. Dina's problems escalated, and she was unable to go to her job interview. She also developed a severe headache and had to go to the emergency room. She felt miserable for what happened, but also because she blamed herself for it.

A closely related Catholic theological virtue is termed *temperance*. It means doing things in moderation.

Mario loves chocolate cake. He could easily eat the whole cake his mother bakes every Sunday, but he learned to restrain himself from eating a big piece. He only eats a two-inch slice. His ability to practice temperance applies to other things in his life such as drinking alcohol, watching TV, and indulging in fatty foods.

People who are good at what they do are self-disciplined. They do their work first and play later. When you watch a tennis match, hitting the ball seems easy to do; but the players spend a lot of time practicing and perfecting their strokes. Concert pianists spend a lot of time in solitude practicing their piano pieces. I am sure they do not always feel like practicing, even if they love what they do, but they use self-discipline to continually improve themselves. They do what they need to do first and do other things later.

If you plan to have a good career, spend your prime time studying. Finish doing your homework before you go out with your friends. Weigh the advantages and disadvantages of what you are doing, then commit yourself to execute your chosen task. If you do your work first, you may actually enjoy your leisure activities more and find it to be even more gratifying. Everything has a cost or consequence. You can develop the habit of doing things that are good for you when you live with self-discipline. Honoré de Balzac wrote, "There is no such thing as a great talent without great willpower."

When my grandson Zachary was four years old, he asked for juice. Rhonda, his nanny, told him, "Drinking juice can ruin your teeth when you drink too much." Zack said, "Give me water then." Zachary had the will to do what was good for him. Sometimes you are confronted with situations where you have to decide which action is better under the given circumstances.

Children may learn self-discipline when things are explained to them and they see the advantages of working or experiencing the discomfort before having fun. When they misbehave, they may learn to correct their behavior by giving them a time out. It is one way to teach them self-discipline.

Stretching
Stretch, Stretch,
reach like the athletes.

Stretch, Stretch,
until it hurts
a little bit.
Do this every day.

When we stretch
to be our best selves,
like chrysanthemums
moving together toward the sun,
day to day—
to grow,
we can someday
be what we want to be.
We can compose
our destiny.

ANTICIPATION

If we could foresee many things before bad things happen, we would be able to avoid much heartache. Painful consequences that happened in my own life could have been prevented if I had been able to anticipate them correctly.

Anticipation is the ability to look beyond the present and foresee the consequences of things. Anticipation is also one of our mature ego defenses. When a painful thing is going to happen in your life, think about it ahead of time and gradually build up your mastery of what will happen. Try to foresee and reflect on your life. But we have to accept, too, that we are imperfect and make mistakes. Hindsight is 20/20, but we do not have 20/20 vision when we are living day to day. On the average, we make mistakes about 20 percent of the time in our decisions. All we can do is accept our life the way it is and make the best of it with gratitude and without regrets.

One of my friends told me that had he paid for his daughter's college tuition, she would have ended up with a college degree and a better job. I told him that we are never perfect and sometimes we make wrong decisions. We cannot live looking back most of the time. We have to make the best of the present, deal with our current problems, and plan for our future. We have to keep walking forward. We cannot walk well when our eyes are looking backward. I made him laugh! We can learn from our mistakes. Wisdom means not repeating the same mistakes.

When you anticipate future discomfort and prepare yourselves for what has to happen, you suffer less. For instance, you cope better when the time comes to have an operation if you prepare yourselves ahead of time. Fewer surgical complications occur when patients are calm—when they have anticipated what they have to go through during surgery and afterward. Their blood pressure and heartbeats are stable. If they are apprehensive and nervous, some surgeons elect to postpone elective surgeries because patients are not psychologically ready. I know of a patient who developed upper gastrointestinal bleeding from being too nervous on the day of her elective surgery.

While doing my physical exercise, I think of how good I am feeling and how good I will be feeling afterward, knowing that I have done one of the most difficult things I need to do for the day. I told some of my patients who love to eat, even when they are not hungry, to associate not eating with feeling good about themselves.

You can also use anticipation to bear your present pain a little more easily by thinking of better days ahead rather than the present discomfort. For example, if you have a busy day at work, think that after that day's hard work, you can go to the beach and have a relaxing time. If you enjoy watching your favorite TV programs, reading magazines, cooking, or window shopping, you can think of these fun activities ahead of time. This can motivate you to do your work. By thinking this way, you can bear your present discomfort better.

Reading the Bible, histories, current events, and biographies is one way to learn more things about life, to become wiser, and to improve your ability to anticipate things. Although each of us is a unique human being, we have stories similar to other people's lives. We can learn from history and apply the lessons others have learned to our lives.

Anticipation

We look to the right and see the shining sun,
to the left, to the front and back appreciating the skies;
then we live in the present
and bear our pain
with a sigh of acceptance.

We can use our best judgment,
applying right and wrong
and anticipate what can happen.
Whatever happens,
as long as we have done
our best, is all right.

When in pain,
we can anticipate the pleasant
days ahead.
We learn
to go through life
like the sun
that keeps on shining.

The more we anticipate
what can happen,

the better decisions we make.
We can change our plans
as minutes go by.

SUBLIMATION (CREATIVITY)

Many roads lead to the same destination. We need to be creative in solving problems and in channeling emotions into constructive activities. Instead of concentrating on upsetting thoughts, I spend my energy doing something for my son by writing. Samantha took up kickboxing to sublimate her anger. In psychiatry, this ego defense is termed *sublimation.*

Creativity, too, is a basic skill or talent. You can use creativity to sublimate your feelings, or you can be a creative person naturally. Some people create something without expressing sublimation to channel their uncomfortable emotions. They just express their creative talent as part of their intelligence.

God created this beautiful world. You can become inspired by communing with nature and absorbing the beauty around you. You can look at beautiful paintings, listen to beautiful music, and watch plays and performances. You can watch inspiring TV programs, and cook meals using creative recipes. Be inspired and use your creativity. Make your environment beautiful. The progress in this world is done by creative people.

Bill Gates changed the world by inventing Microsoft Windows. Henry Ford started to manufacture cars for mass production by designing an assembly line. Steve Jobs was instrumental in inventing and designing many things, including the iMac, iPhone, and iTunes.

Our creative power comes from our soul. It is an expression of our individuality. When we create something, we express beauty, truth, or goodness that can help and inspire people. (We can also create things that can be harmful and dangerous.)

John Keats wrote, "A thing of beauty is a joy forever." What you create is something that makes you happy and brings joy to your lives. No one can take that away from you. You carry it anywhere and everywhere you go.

Creative work can be anything you see as the best course of action or solution to problems. You can express your creativity when you solve day-to-day problems or by engaging in simple activities, such as arranging closets, cooking, or scheduling. You can sing, dance, write, paint, do arts and crafts, arrange your apartment, and so on.

An old man and a young man happened to be sitting on a bench in the park. The young man said, "You know, all you old people do not understand us because we live in a different age. We have computers, iPads, helicopters, and motorcycles."

The old man was quiet and then said, "We made these things happen in your generation. What are you creating for the next generation?"

Memories of Edward
There are many happy memories.
Every single second shared.

There were thoughts filled with dreams,
Even when dreams were cut short,
They were vivid dreams,
These are happy memories.

They are the treasures in my heart,
They are the colors in my mind,
The sudden rainbows that stay.

These are the beautiful things in my life.
These are my happy memories.

Sublimation
We can channel
Our emotions

And express them
Constructively like
Oysters creating pearls
From a grain of sand.

We can transform
Our socially unacceptable
Behaviors at the moment
And do beautiful things.

Create
Look!
Find the best way to solve
your tasks, small and big.
Ask God for guidance
to make you see things better.

Think!
Write your solutions.
Make them constructive to yourself
and to others.

Play!
Make new things.
Let them glitter like the stars.
Let your solutions
flow like waterfalls.

Dream!
But be disciplined.
Imagine the possible,
although it can be fun
to dream the impossible.

Dreams
Dreams are beautiful things;
Small, big, fleeting, lasting,

We wish for ourselves,
For the people we love.

Dreams sometimes come true!
Our eyes glitter, our pupils big, our lives fulfilled.
Sometimes dreams remain like clouds in the sky;
Our eyes strained, our pupils small, our lives
incomplete.

We have to touch our dreams
With our hearts
While we keep our feet
With multi-colored sandals on the ground
And walk.

When we forget, intentionally, unintentionally,
We think our dreams are real,
Like living with sunshine and moon,
When they are only dreams, just movies in our minds,
We live as misplaced luggage
In another planet.

Waiting
Some of our time
is spent waiting—
waiting
at the counter,
for traffic;
waiting
as the white thin
hungry heron
waits
on the edge
of the pond.

Be like the moon
waiting for dawn.

Creativity
We will see new ways
of doing things like children
gathering twigs and leaves
to make pictures.

We can try
doing new things
combining things in a new way
until beautiful
or simple
or noble,
or true
things form.

Writing
I write to remember
I write to forget
I write to be in touch with my feelings
I write to quiet my feelings.
What I write
I can re-write
As I re-write my life.

I am happy when I write
My spirit beams with joy
I feel so alive
Like morning glories
That suddenly bloom.

Humor

Life is difficult. If you can find something to laugh about, in many situations you can lighten your burdens. Laughter releases endorphins, which are chemicals in the brain that make us feel good and lessen our pains. We can even laugh at ourselves.

When my grandson Zachary was four, I heard him play a harmonica for the first time. I was impressed and joyfully asked him, "What are you playing, Zack?" He answered, "Jarmonica." I asked him again, and he answered, "Jarmonica." I asked my daughter, Melin, and she answered, "Jarmonica." Zachary then said, "Grandma, that's what I was telling you!" I laughed as I finally realized that I am a little deaf and have problems hearing some sounds correctly.

My son-in-law, David, asked Zachary his age. He said, "Four." David then said, "It's Grandma's birthday. How old do you think Grandma is?" Zack answered, "Ten." David said, "Older." Zack then said, "Fourteen."

I have the privilege of spending time with my grandsons once a week. For two months, when my grandson Emmett Edward was one year old, his favorite word was *more*. It meant that he wanted more food. Two months later, his favorite words became *no more*.

Zachary was in the kitchen assembling his new toy. He heard something fall on the floor and heard Emmett in the living room crying. He immediately announced, "I didn't do it."

Both children are happy, animated, exuberant, and playful. Given a chance, spend time with children; they will certainly enrich your sense of humor.

I practice internal medicine. My patients ask me, "How long have you been practicing, Doc?" "Forty years," I answer. They uniformly say, "Wow! You look good!" (Everybody is doing the math.)

Bishop Fulton J. Sheen, in his old age, told his friend Norman Vincent Peale that there are three ages of men: "Youth, middle age, and my, but you look good."

Whatever difficulties you have in life, you are able to handle them better when you live with a sense of humor because humor is one of our mature ego defenses. Often, when painful, disappointing, or sad things happen in my life, I ask myself, "Do you want to cry or do you want to laugh?" I keep a notebook of funny occurrences and read them when I have a hectic day. To do so brightens my day. Sometimes, I watch a rerun of *I Love Lucy* or reread humorist Erma Bombeck's books. I also watch the television comedy *Everybody Loves Raymond*. One of my close friends sends me humorous stories and short movie clips through my e-mail.

I have a patient-friend who comes to the office with jokes all the time. We both have big smiles even before she sits down.

I just read an article that said C. S. Lewis had a great sense of humor, too. Humor helped him cope with the ordeal of taking care of his wife and eventually losing her from cancer.

Arthur went to his barber for a haircut and he told him that he was planning to go to Rome to see the pope. The barber said, "Don't take Alitalia airline. It's very crowded, and the seats are narrow. And I do not think you will be able to see the pope. The Vatican is very crowded." The following week, Arthur came back and told the barber, "I had the best trip ever. The airplane was spacious and comfortable. I saw the pope, and he came right up to me and whispered, 'Where did you get your horrible haircut?'"

Humor (One)
Pilar, do you feel
like crying?
I know the skies have fallen
on top of your head.

Laugh, laugh until you feel better;
until the skies will move back—
high up.
Pilar, when you feel really sad,
laugh. Let your sadness go to the clouds
like loaves of bread

at the Bread Loaf skies
in Vermont.

Let laughter clean all the chambers of your heart;
clean your veins, arteries, and lymphatic system.

Laugh and dance, tap your thymus gland;
it is underneath your sternum.
Sing one of your favorite songs,
"Tomorrow."

Pilar, laugh!
Don't make passing things permanent,
let them pass
like a heavy rain.

Pilar, laugh!
The pains
that never go away
only make you stronger.
They add strength
to the fibers of your heart.

Humor   (Two)
Whatever comes,
whatever happens,
just laugh.
Let laughter
be like the air
you breathe.

Accept
life's
frequent changes
like sun and rain,
cold and hot
during the day;
and

the constantly
changing moon,
the changing
visibility of the stars
at night.

Besides learning and using mature ego defenses, you need to become holy in order to strengthen your emotional maturity. The word *holy* comes from the Anglo-Saxon word *wholth*, which means wholeness. Our heart and soul have to be whole to be mature.

CHAPTER 2

❖

Journey to Holiness

Holiness is not just a doctrine, it is a
way of life—it is the life of Jesus.
—Duncan Campbell

T HE FIRST TWO secrets from the apparition of Fatima, which
concern the conversion of Russia and the fall of the Berlin
Wall, were revealed in the early part of the twentieth century.
Reading about them strengthens my faith in God and in the
Blessed Virgin Mary. It is an inspiration to know the third and
last secret of Fatima.

The Blessed Virgin Mary appeared in Fatima, Portugal, in
1917, to three children: Lucia, Francisco, and Jacinta. Sister Lucia
was the last of the three children to die. She was born in March
28, 1907, and died on February 13, 2005, at age ninety-seven.
She lived a cloistered life in a Carmelite monastery in Coimbra,
Portugal. She wrote the third secret of the apparition in Fatima
by the order of His Excellency, the Bishop of Leiria, Fatima, on
January 3, 1941. It was later published with the permission of
Pope John Paul II.

According to Sister Lucia, the Blessed Virgin Mary told her: For
us to be close to God, we should follow the Ten Commandments
and keep praying, in order that we may have peace in this world.
You can search for "Vatican message of Fatima" on the Internet
for more detail.

FAITH IN GOD

Because of the traumatic experience of losing my beloved son, I sometimes worry. I worry that perhaps something very painful will happen again in my life to those I deeply love. Thoughts just come, but I do not dwell on them. My antidote to these anxious feelings and thoughts is my faith in God. I submit to God's will for my life. I pray. I pray all the time that my son Edward is supremely happy with God.

In February 2011, I had the same dream of Edward twice. He was in his favorite Bermuda shorts, relaxed and walking close to a well in a beautiful park—the same well that I had seen when I visited Fatima in Portugal. In his book *Interpretation of Dreams*, Carl Jung wrote that our dreams are God's gifts to us. Since having that dream, I intuitively know that Edward is with God. He is in a better, peaceful, and beautiful place. Experiencing that dream gave me peace, comfort, and joy. I still continuously pray for him as I constantly remember him. I carry him in my thoughts and heart always. God, my guardian angels, my favorite saints, and Edward are my daily companions.

Several times a day, depending on my schedule, I meditate on the Lord's Prayer. (See Appendix B.) I also pray and say the novena to the infant Jesus of Prague, whom we call Santo Niño (Holy Child) in the Philippines. Santo Niño is the patron saint of our neighborhood. My parents donated a piece of land and money to build a chapel there and named our chapel Santo Niño. When I visited our barrio two years ago, my niece had a big statue of Santo Niño right in front of the chapel.

Many parishioners told me stories that the Santo Niño statue disappears at night to roam around and comes back in place during the day. According to them, the Santo Niño had performed many miracles. One of my regrets in life was my not asking the Santo Niño to specifically keep Edward from any harm while he was still living. I know that things happen for a reason that I cannot understand, and that everything that happens comes from the will of God, but I cannot help thinking that perhaps I could have done something to prevent the tragedy from happening.

I am not sure if I believe that the Santo Niño disappears at night. I think it is just a superstition, but I believe that the Santo Niño has been performing miracles there. The Philippines has 7,108 islands during low tide and 7,107 islands during high tide. Only two thousand islands are inhabited. In Cebu City, the oldest city on one island, not the one I came from, people celebrate the fiesta of Santo Niño the third week of January. Devotion to the Infant Jesus of Prague was brought by the Spaniards in 1565 to Mactan Island, a part of Cebu. The church burned to the ground, but the statue remained intact and was proclaimed miraculous.

The fiesta of Santo Niño is simultaneously celebrated in many other islands in the Philippines as well. People wear costumes, have dance contests, and dance and parade with the Santo Niño on the streets during the three-day yearly celebration. Before the street affairs begin, there is a nine-day novena.

I just gave my second Santo Niño (I had two) to my secretary-extended family, Jenny, and told her that the statue was an exact replica of the Santo Niño in our barrio. I also told her, "This Infant Jesus might disappear at night."

I have been saying the rosary every day since Edward died. (See Appendix B.) The Blessed Virgin Mary is our national patron. We Filipinos call her "Mama Mary." We believe that in 1948, she had an apparition in Lipa City, located in Luzon, the island where Manila is located. Her message was about reciting the rosary for peace.

I was raised in the Roman Catholic Church. Sometimes I attend other Christian churches, those in which I feel a sense of belonging and those that have excellent homilies. I believe in the Holy Trinity, and I pray for the Holy Spirit to guide me. I thank God for the blessings He gives me, and I ask God for protection, guidance, and enlightenment to make me do what I ought to do in my life.

I have been reading about the world's religions: Islam, Buddhism, Taoism, Hinduism, Christianity, and Judaism. I am convinced that all religions can be good for people. Religion gives us guidance, strength, and guideposts for constructive living, as well as a broader knowledge and understanding about life. It can help us accept tragedies and suffering and can lead us to peace. Religion leads us to believe that there is life after our body dies.

The Bible's writing is the best companion for my daily life. There are many publications derived from the Bible. You can go to Christian book stores, churches, websites, and libraries or ask your friends for recommendations. I am currently reading Catholic Bible companion books sent by my sister from the Philippines. My favorite book is still the original Bible, containing the Old and New Testaments. I have also read many books on different Christian denominations. Like the Roman Catholic teachings, they have some individual rules and different ways of explaining the scriptures, but their basic teachings are the same. They are: to have faith in God, have a personal relationship with God, accept and do God's will, and be a good and loving person.

A friend sent this to me:

WHO SHOULD READ THE BIBLE
The Young- To learn how to live.
The Old- To know how to die.
The Ignorant- For wisdom.
The Learned- For humility.
The Rich- For compassion.
The Poor- For comfort.
The Dreamer- For enchantment.
The Practical- For counsel.
The Weak- For strength.
The Strong- For direction.
The Haughty- For warning.
The Humble- For exaltation.
The Troubled- For peace.

The Weary- For rest.
The Doubting- For assurance.
The Sinner- For salvation.
The Christian- For guidance.
                    —Author Unknown

You need to respect people for their own beliefs about the world regardless of the kind of religion you practice. Even if you do not practice any religion at all, you can be open to other people's beliefs and teachings. I know some people who did not believe in any God when they were young, but as they lived longer they became spiritual. Some even became religious.

Most people practice the religion in which we were raised. There are many vantage points in terms of looking at and interpreting life's events. Group Bible studies, reading guidebooks, and listening to good preachers are ways of broadening our knowledge of God's Word.

There are many paths to God. Joan Borysenko, PhD, wrote that there are seven paths to God. It is good to keep reading and studying the Bible throughout your lifetime. The Psalms guide us in our relationship with God; the Proverbs guide us in our relationships with ourselves, our family, friends, and the world.

Here is a research study funded by the Pew Charitable Trust:

Total world population in 2010—6.9 billion
84% (5.8 billion) have religious affiliations
16% (1.1 billion) have no particular faith or religious affiliation, but most believe in God or universal spirit, these include atheist and/or agnostic.

32% (2.2 billion) are Christians—(1.1 billion) are Catholics
23 % (1.6 billion) are Muslims
15% (1 billion) are Hindus
7% (nearly 500 million) are Buddhists
0.2% (14 million) believe in Judaism

Almost everybody who believes in God prays to God. How we pray differs depending on our religious affiliations, but in general we ask God for guidance, forgiveness, help, and mercy.

As we mature and become responsible for ourselves, our worldview can also change. Some people are able to integrate and practice some beliefs that originated from different religions. I have Catholic, Judeo-Christian beliefs, and also believe in reincarnation, or life after life. I believe that our soul or spirit (I consider soul and spirit as the same) lives forever after our physical death, but God wants us to reincarnate back to earth as another physical being to grow spiritually as needed, not as a lower form of animal, as Hindus and Buddhists believe.

My view on reincarnation and my other religious beliefs might change as I grow intellectually. It's just as Ralph Waldo Emerson wrote: "I wish to say what I think and feel today, with the provision that tomorrow perhaps I shall contradict it all."

I have a patient-friend who practices Orthodox Judaism. She, too, believes in reincarnation. She told me that this is a Jewish belief called *gilgul*. I believe that God lets us return to earth to complete our mission and that our souls go to heaven permanently after we have lived a good life.

It is interesting that Pearl S. Buck, who was raised as a Presbyterian (her father was a Presbyterian missionary in China), believed in Buddhism.

The current Dalai Lama was born in 1935 to a peasant family in northeastern Tibet. His birth name was Tenzin Gyatzo. He was recognized at two years old as the reincarnation of his predecessor, the thirteenth Dalai Lama.

There are many books on reincarnation. My favorites are books written by Brian Weiss, MD, entitled *Many Lives, Many Masters*, and Gary Zukav's *The Seat of the Soul*.

Dr. Weiss is a psychiatrist. He wrote about his interviews with his patients recounting their past life experiences under hypnosis.

He was able to document current emotional problems originating from the patients' previous lives.

Gary Zukav's book is about evolution, and also reincarnation. It is about having nonphysical guides and teachers. Zukav discusses the qualities of the soul, such as harmony, cooperation, sharing, and reverence for life, and its authentic power.

I believe that we are supposed to suffer in this life as Jesus Christ suffered and died on the cross, but I also practice detachment as one way of helping me cope with the pains that come with living. The broader our knowledge about many things, the more resources we have in handling our lives.

I hope that someday all houses of worship will acknowledge that they are all part of one universal house. Whether we believe in one God or many gods, we can unite as one universal house of worship; we are all part of planet Earth. I have witnessed pride and prejudice in people, insisting that their religion is the only true and right religion. Some Christians also insist that their particular church is the only true church because it was founded by Jesus Christ. We should not fight and hate people for practicing a religion different from our own. We should have an open mind and respect each other's beliefs. It is good to love enough to allow people to be who and what they choose to be. Love is allowing persons to be what they are and not what we think they should be. Abraham Maslow wrote, "What a man can be, he must be." There are many religions and many Gods and gods. Joseph Campbell wrote about this in his book *The Hero with a Thousand Faces*. Right now, religion divides people. We will have a greater chance to have peace on earth when we can unite our houses of worship as one regardless of the specific religion we practice.

On October 7, 2010, I was watching Diane Sawyer on *World News*. A survey showed that nine out of ten Americans believe in God; 28 percent believe in an authoritative and judgmental God; 22 percent believe in a benevolent and loving God; 21 percent believe in a critical God; and 28 percent believe in a God that set the world in motion and then disengaged from it. I personally believe in a loving and merciful God.

One of the miners who was trapped after the earthquake in Chile in April 2010 said, "I never learned to pray; but down there, I learned to pray." Faith is developed at various times and circumstances. Eric Fromm wrote, "Faith doesn't wait until it understands, in that case it wouldn't be faith." St. Augustine also wrote, "Faith is to believe what we do not see; and the reward of this faith is to see what we believe."

I acquired my faith by learning Catholic prayers in Latin while young. I lived the first six years of my life on a farm owned by my grandfather. A farmer's wife, who was about fifty years old at that time, taught me how to pray the rosary in Latin. As far as I can remember, I have always believed in God, and my mother spent at least one hour each day kneeling and praying. Whether good things or bad things happened in our lives, she would always say, "This is all God's will." Our house in the city burned to the ground when I was eight years old. We lost every material thing, but my parents took the disaster as part of life and God's will. I was born during the Japanese invasion in the Philippines. I grew up with tragic war and postwar stories. Every day, my mother reminded us to thank God for our health and blessings.

However, I did not know any Bible stories and did not read the Bible until I came to America and started reading my children's books. I studied at a high school, in a special class run by a Catholic order of nuns called the Order of St. Columba, originally from Ireland, but I only learned a few prayers and some choir songs. We did not use any books in class, and I did not borrow any books or use our school library. Even at home we did not have religious books. I remember my father had philosophy books. He graduated with a degree in philosophy in China and taught school in the Philippines, where he met my mother. But all the books were burned during the fire that destroyed our home.

I consider myself to be deeply spiritual, but not committed to practicing just one organized Christian religion. I disagree with some teachings and rules of the Roman Catholic Church, as I also disagree with some teachings and rules of other Christian churches. After exploring other religions, I like the Catholic religion the most, since I believe in the Holy Trinity, the Blessed Virgin Mary, the saints, and miracles. And it is the religion that has had more influence in my life. I also have an affinity for the Jewish religion since my grandchildren are being raised Jewish.

I have a personal relationship with Jesus Christ. I think of myself as a strong believer in Jesus Christ. I know that Jesus Christ is the son of God, my redeemer. I believe that the Holy Spirit is within us and gives us spiritual blessings such as love, joy, peace, goodness, happiness, meekness, long-suffering, self-discipline, wisdom, knowledge, faith, healing, miraculous powers, and prophecy. It enables us to distinguish between spirits, to speak in tongues, and to interpret what was spoken in tongues. I attended a Pentecostal service one time, and my patient-friend spoke in tongues. I called her on the phone afterward, and she explained to me that another person next to her wrote what she was saying and recognized it as Italian, a language my patient-friend had never learned before.

This is what I experience when I think about God:

God is life. When we are alive in this world, we are living with God—we can be fully functioning and open to all that life brings. Unfortunately, we often close ourselves to life's possibilities, and we then spend our time thinking about destructive thoughts or feelings such as fear, envy, and anger. Instead of being engaged with life, we feel depressed and may do nothing. When we are full of life, we are usually healthy and function well.

God is love. Heaven is love. Jesus Christ said, "For behold, the kingdom of God is among you." (Luke 17:21, *New American Bible*) Love is within us. When we live with love, we live with joy, although there is a possibility of loss and pain that goes with love. God gave Moses the Ten Commandments. The first three are about loving God; the remaining seven are about loving our neighbors as ourselves. Living as a good person and developing our character is the main purpose of our temporary life here on earth. Although the Ten Commandments are instructions on what to do and what not to do in this world, the outcome of following the Ten Commandments is love. We are here on earth to learn how to love. Sophocles wrote, "One word frees us of the weight and pain in life; that word is love." We can live by the golden rule, "Do unto others as you would have others do unto you." I believe Jesus Christ is our guide and role model for living. Currently, I am studying the Jewish religion because my grandsons are practicing and learning it. Those of the Jewish faith do not believe in Jesus Christ as the Messiah and their guide and role model for living. They believe that the Messiah as predicted by the prophets in the Old Testament is still to come. Nevertheless, Judaism values love.

God is spirit. God is indestructible, unchanging, and permanent. God lives forever. Spirit can never die. Like God, we are born with a spirit. Our spirit lives forever. Our body dies and decays, but our spirit lives on. Like the stories of the book of Revelation, in the Christian New Testament—our life here on earth can be full of pain, tragedy, and destruction. We can accept suffering as our reality because we know that there is a better life after we die physically, if we repent our sins and live a good life now.

Everything here on earth is temporary. Pain and pleasure pass. The world is constantly changing. This is brilliantly shown with the drawing of the Tao, which shows the imperfection of life by having a black or negative part in the white or positive part; and a white or positive part in a mainly black or negative part. The Tao is constantly moving. In this drawing, the black part eventually becomes the white part and vice versa.

Tao (pronounced "dow") originated in China. Lao-tzu, about five hundred years before Christ, wrote the *Tao Te Ching* (pronounced "dow day jing"), describing it as "the Book of the Way." It was written as unassertive action and philosophy, but later practiced as a religion.

Yin and yang, the positive and negative, are constantly moving and changing. They have varying parts of each other, always together but varying in their quantity. Yin and yang illustrate the impermanence, imperfection, and duality of life, as well as the complementary aspects of life. Yin and yang have opposite qualities, as explained in the book *Understanding the I Ching,* by Cyrille Javay.

yin	yang
feminine	masculine
dark	light
cold	hot
low	high
night	day
interior	exterior
rest	action

Rick Warren, author of *The Purpose Driven Life* and pastor of Saddlebrook Church in California, said during his interview by Paul Bradshaw that he believes that life is like two rails on a railroad track. At all times you have something good and something bad in your life. No matter how good things are, there is always something bad that needs to be addressed. No matter how bad things are, there is always something good for which you can thank God. His view is like the Tao's belief in the imperfection, duality, and impermanence of our life here on earth.

We are here to learn our lessons, to grow, to complete, to make personal sacrifices, to make this world a better place, to find meaning in our suffering, to purify our souls, to become holy, and to love better. I learned from my own spirituality that the Holy Spirit lives in us. In church, we are given the gifts and the fruits of the Holy Spirit when we are baptized as followers of Jesus Christ. The gifts of the Holy Spirit are wisdom, understanding, right judgment, courage, knowledge, reverence, and wonder and awe in God's presence. The fruits of the Holy Spirit are peace, joy, love, kindness, patience, self-control, gentleness, goodness, long-suffering, faith, chastity, and modesty. When we pray, we can ask the Holy Spirit, who dwells within us, to make us conscious of God's gifts and fruits. When we become Christians, we commit to love God and follow Jesus Christ's teachings every day, not just occasionally or whenever we feel like it.

God is one. God is neither masculine nor feminine. God is undivided and cannot be broken into parts. Our spirit or soul is the essence of our being, like the extract of a flower. It is who we are, our character. When we have love in our soul, we are one with God.

God is intelligence. Possibly because of original sin, there is so much evil, tragedy, and suffering in this world. But there is no real answer for "why bad things happen to good people." I trust that things happen for a reason. We may not know the reasons why things happen the way they do, but we achieve peace and accept reality because we know that God has a divine plan for our life and for the world.

Synchronicity and serendipity happen in life. Good fortune is a common occurrence. Bad fortune also happens. I have had some good fortune and bad fortune that's happened in my life. One of my friends claims that 60 percent of our life depends on ourselves and 40 percent depends on other factors such as our heredity, the parents who raised us, and what country we are living in.

God is truth, and truth heals us. We can pray for divine guidance to bring us truth. Wherever there is truth, there is God. Reading and studying the Bible, the Quran, or the Bhagavad Gita can lead us to see truth or God. Meditation, contemplation, and being with nature can make us experience and know truth. Art is truth expressed by artists to enrich this world. Sacred writings are truth written in many forms, ways, and times; but they are timeless and the same.

God is permanent. God is the same forever. God is forever our God. We accept what God is. We experience God, but we do not question God's plan for our lives and the world. If we question them, chances are we will not come up with acceptable answers. From the biblical scholar's point of view, the words of God were experienced by people and then communicated orally or in writing. As we grow, we have the opportunity to understand the Bible in a deeper and more meaningful way. The words of God have not changed, but we can change our interpretation as we become more enlightened and wiser. Who and what we have become influences the way we see and understand things.

God has the power to do anything and everything. I am aware that there are many things I do not know about God; but I think miracles, spiritual healing, and answered prayers come from God. In my observation, all prayerful people practicing their religions have a more positive attitude, peace and acceptance in their lives, and they live longer than people who are not devoted to God or do not believe in God.

Having faith in God is a gift from God. Intellectual people who question the presence of God almost always end up believing in God. Albert Einstein believed in God. Some people may not label God as God, but they believe in something supernatural.

We should make the effort to cultivate our spirituality. We can expose ourselves to spiritual things. Lord Acton, who was a peer of the United Kingdom from 1869 to 1902, appointed the Regius professorship of modern history at Cambridge, was one of the most deeply learned men of his time. He was a Roman Catholic. And *The Cambridge Modern History*, though he did not live to see it, was planned under his editorship. He wrote, "To a symmetrical nature religion is indeed a crown of glory, nevertheless, so far as this world is concerned, they can grow and prosper without it. But to the unsymmetrical nature religion is a necessary condition of successful work even in this world." Lord Acton's writing means that if our life is going well and balanced, does not have tragic occurrences, we do not need any religion to prosper, it will just be a big bonus. But, if our lives are too difficult to accept, we need religion in order to survive with acceptance and peace in ourselves.

Here is a prayer shared by a friend. It is similar to an ancient Hawaiian practice of forgiveness and reconciliation performed traditionally by the kahuna lapa'au, a Hawaiian Huna priest, but anyone can perform the modern variation.

"I am sorry, Lord.
Forgive me, Lord.
Thank you, Lord.
I love you, Lord."

I have been saying this prayer every hour for nine hours almost every day ever since my friend shared it with me. Saying it throughout the day is an effective way of communing with God, having a short time to relax and meditate, just as those who practice Islam say their prayers five times a day. I also say this prayer to myself and for the people with whom I interact. Saying a prayer every hour also makes me more aware of how I live my life and how I spend my time each day.

Going through heart surgery, my friend prayed, "Sacred heart of Jesus, I trust in you." We can talk to God in our own way. We can say what we want to say to God. We can pray to thank God for blessings, to contemplate and commune with God, to ask for graces, for guidance, for enlightenment, for strength, or for anything and everything, like conversing with our true friend.

Faith

There is always somebody
who is there for me
day and night
when the roses bloom,
when the violets rest,
when the sand blows
in the wind.

We are restless as the winds,
incomplete
as a lock without a key;
until we recognize God,
until we have faith in God.

Edward wrote,
"I've met God in several places,
seen God in several people,
but my most personal experience
of God
comes from being out in the water,
riding the waves."

My dream for the rest of my life
is to do God's will;
to be and do my best,
to always have love in my heart,
to have eternal life with God.

After the sad telephone call
My mind went over
the things
I've learned
through the years—
pathophysiology, anatomy,
rationale, medications;
flashbacks of patients
I have treated, people
I have known, sceneries,
successes, and heartaches.

Hours went by
without any brilliant
ideas shining through.
I consciously
stopped my thoughts
and experienced awe
at the wonders
of each moment—
dark skies with dots
of stars, orchids in the forest,
islands with incredibly beautiful beaches,
birds singing; I felt God
and knew that miracles
are everywhere.

Faith is many
magnificent things.
It is the sun and stars in summer,
fall, spring, especially in winter.

Facts about medicine
There are things besides medicine
that make people well;
the spirit within a person,
the grace from God.
There are things besides medicine

that control our destiny.
Sometimes very ill people
recover and get well
against all scientific odds.

Have faith in ourselves
and our God to be well.

We can learn about nutrition,
exercise, meditation; spiritual,
emotional, and physical healing.

After we have done our part
we can then leave
everything to God.

CHARACTER AND DEVELOPMENT OF VALUES

Our morality goes hand in hand with our emotional maturity.
When we are taught the Ten Commandments before we become
mature emotionally, we do not automatically become moral.
Instead, we only develop guilt because we do not automatically
follow the commandments. To love God and to love our neighbor
as ourselves takes maturity, work, discipline, and will. It takes
wisdom to become a good person. We are born sinners. We need to
educate ourselves through observations, self-reflections, studying
religions, studying great literature, continuous prayers, and having
intimate relationships, to eventually become a good person and to
realize that the Ten Commandments are God's gift to us.

It is a good habit to reflect every day and to ask God for
forgiveness for the things that we did that were wrong and for
the things that we failed to do. I do not go to church every day
and I do not go to confession regularly, but Matthew Kelly's
book titled *Rediscover Catholicism* convinced me of the benefits of
practicing these religious habits in one's life. We lighten our load

in life when we repent for our sins and spend time communicating with God regularly.

There are values by which we need to live to have a good life and be a good person. There are also values that change over time as we change. The following are some of the good characteristics and values we can develop in ourselves to become our best selves:

- Humility—We are not proud or arrogant. We can be real and sincere human beings.
- Self-discipline—We can control our destructive thoughts, feelings and actions. We can will or choose to do to what we think, what we feel, and what we do. We can be proactive instead of reactive.
- Compassion—We suffer when other people suffer. We help whoever and whatever we can.
- Forgiveness—We easily forgive ourselves and others.
- Empathy—We can experience what another person is feeling.
- Moderation—We can do and have things that are appropriate; there is a happy medium.
- Positive mental attitude—We can look at the good side of things and see the advantages for every disadvantage.
- Truthfulness—We can be true to ourselves and live and share our truth.
- Respect—We treat everyone with esteem and as unique individuals.
- Peacefulness–We have faith and trust in God's will for our lives.
- Generosity—We give whatever we can to better the world for people, such as by protecting animals and the environment, and preventing war.
- Industry—We work hard and use our energy constructively.
- Prayerfulness—All things are possible when we pray. We raise our minds and hearts to God when we pray. We

commune with God and make prayer a way of life. God can make miracles happen, and we accept God's will for us.

- Orderliness—Our life becomes simpler and easier to manage when we are orderly.
- We love God, and love our neighbors as ourselves—We aspire to be good human beings.

Some of these things we learn well while growing up. Others we have to acquire and develop as we live day to day. In my practice as an internist, I experienced that people who are centered on God, regardless of their religions, follow the above values to live by. I have Christian, Muslim, Buddhist, and Jewish patients who are all good people.

There are cultural values that we acquire through our environment. Growing up in the Philippines, surrounded by extreme poverty, it was customary for us to share and help our family and community. We were hospitable and entertained people with food—whoever came to our home to visit. We even gave up our bedrooms for our visitors. We also had great respect for our elders. We served them food first. My friend who noticed our culture mentioned to me that here in America, children are fed first before older people.

I have to discipline myself to keep my home and workplace neat and orderly. It makes life easier when we keep what we have in designated places.

I learned to work hard from my parents' examples and later, during my college years, from my dormmates. We studied first before we played or told stories. I loved to learn things, and I was curious about several things in life, especially plants and flowers. I used to pick leaves and flowers and dry them by putting them inside my notebooks. My favorite college course was botany.

Things that are important to us may change as we age. Usually, we realize as we get older that material things and outward success are not as important as inner success. We value spiritual things more as we live longer. This is the wisdom we develop as we live and grow. Our authentic life is more important than outward things.

However, there is wisdom we can learn early in life. Growing up, my father encouraged me to grow intellectually and spiritually, to be intellectually and emotionally self-reliant, to have compassion and charity, and do my best. He also told parables to show me the importance of sharing and giving back to the community to make a difference in peoples' lives.

I became intellectually self-reliant in my teens. I have changed over the years, but my parents' teachings stayed with me. I admired and appreciated them more as I got older. They used to say, "Do whatever you want in life as long as you are true to yourself, charitable, and are responsible. Remember also that you pay a price for your choices in life."

HIGHER CONSCIOUSNESS (GOD- LOVE)

If we want to be continuously happy and joyful in this world, we have to practice unconditional love, which is God or love consciousness. We have to practice unconditional love the way it ought to be: unchanging and permanent, a state of being that has purity of motive; compassionate, nurturing and forgiving. It is not easy for us to reach this level of consciousness, but we can make this our aim in life. We can influence people by our examples. Our effort will improve not only our own lives, it may also elevate humanity.

Suffering does not take away our happiness. Even when we are suffering, we can still be happy. Happiness, like love, is a state of being. We can be happy regardless of the sufferings we undergo in life.

I have the privilege of knowing somebody who is always happy. She has an invalid son who needs constant medical care. He had been in and out of the hospital, and his mother has had to deal with so many problems, but she is happy. It is a pleasure to be around her because she concentrates on and talks about other things, not about her problems.

Some people have chronic illnesses early in their lives. They live with handicaps, chronic pain, and disabilities; and yet they live happy lives. They find advantages from their disadvantages. It is not what we cannot do that matters; it is what we do with what we have and our attitude that makes a difference in our lives.

Unconditional love can release endorphins. When we are loving, we have positive thoughts. Some literature suggests that just thinking good thoughts can release endorphins. (See http://www.billtontzjrmd.com.) It can even heal our illnesses. This may be one reason why spiritual people are generally healthier than the general population. People who achieve unconditional love radiate positive energy. We feel good around them.

> **Unconditional Love (Two)**
> Do good things for yourself,
> unconditional love is the nutrient you need to be
> happy and joyful.
> Do good things for others,
> give them flowers for their soul.
> Help heal their pains, their fears,
> shame, guilt, anger, and destructive cravings.
>
> Do whatever you can, even small things, each day.
> Peace, joy, happiness, and love
> are bouquets of flowers in your heart.
>
> Put love in your hands,
> blow it like bubbles
> that are carried by the winds.
> Let love grow
> wild as the trees
> for everyone
> to share like the air we breathe.

Meditate on these:

- Meditate on the description of love.
- Meditate on loving yourself by applying the description of love.
- Meditate on loving everyone for the love of God; think of the divinity within them.

Love is	Loving yourself	Loving everyone for the love of God
A decision		
Unconditional		
Courageous		
Effort-filled		
Patient		
Kind		
Forgiving		
Humble		
Unselfish		
Not arrogant or rude		
Empathetic		
Never ending		

There is a difference between loving yourself and being a self-centered or selfish person. Loving yourself means being good to yourself, doing what is constructive for yourself and others; not thinking and doing for yourself at the other's expense or doing for yourself without regard for others.

In essence, self-love is being a good person.

I became closer to God after Edward died. My intuition told me that God would heal me, but I did not know exactly how. So I spent more time reading spiritual books, especially the New Testament. And learning more about God made me become closer to God. We can never know God on this earth, but we can learn a lot about God. I believe God healed me and helped me find peace. I have accepted the pain of losing Edward as part of my life.

Some people lose their sense of God when confronted by tragedy. God is always within them, but the pain and life's trials make them unaware of God's presence in their lives.

Josefa's fifteen-year-old daughter ran away from home and has been missing for over a year. Josefa lost her faith in God. I asked her, "Who do you turn to for help?" She said, "Nobody. I do not believe in God anymore; that's the end of this nonsense, I mean God and saints." I told her that when life becomes more difficult, we need God more. She said, "I know you want to help me, but I do not need your help."

Our soul or the love inside us can sometimes be covered by painful experiences that we are unable to heal. We feel the love and peace in our hearts only when we heal our pain.

Contemplative prayers can get rid of our negative emotions such as pride, anger, fear, greed, lust, sloth, and gluttony; these are capital sins that are buried in our unconscious. Through contemplation, we process our negative emotions, heal ourselves, and listen to what God wants us to do with our lives.

I recently got a telephone call from Josefa, thanking me for sending her the booklet titled *Silent prayer or Contemplative prayer*, by Sr. Mary Niere, OCD. I told her to use it every day.

We experience the ultimate happiness and joy that we can achieve in this world when we reach our highest level of consciousness or spirituality. Regardless of our marital status, socio-economic level, race, or age, we can continue to grow spiritually throughout our lifetime and work hard to make this world a better place for humanity.

These are some ways you may achieve union with God or develop spirituality:

- Read and study the Bible or any religious books from your religious tradition.
- Practice meditation. There are many kinds of meditation: Zen meditation, centering, contemplation, breathing

relaxation exercises, chanting, and praying with beads are some practices. Read and try out some meditation DVD or audio tapes. I am using Wayne Dyer's audio tape, *Meditation for Manifesting*. You can also practice yoga as a way of nonattachment and being in touch with your soul.

- Appreciate and experience beauty and truth. You are surrounded by beauty everywhere. There is nothing as beautiful as the nature that surrounds you, such as trees, flowers, seas, skies, stars, moon, sun, birds, and butterflies. If you are confined to a room and have no access to nature, you can look at pictures, paintings and even imagine or visualize beautiful things. You can also watch television or listen to the radio. I have a patient who made scrapbooks of her happy occasions, and she looked at them frequently. Another patient has pictures of her grandchildren in her wallet and looks at them several times a day. It is their way of remembering God's presence in their lives.

- Experience truth through intuitions, by reading great literature, and from reflection. Learn from these activities that there is a God—a unifying force governing this world.

- Have a passion for helping others. Living a life of service to humanity brings you closer to God.

- Surrender to God and love the world as an expression of your love of God.

- Accept suffering.

ACCEPTANCE OF SUFFERING

Suffering, like death, is one of our human conditions. When, what, and how we suffer varies individually. Nevertheless, all of us suffer at one time or another, even those who die early in life. Some people suffer physically or emotionally all of the time. From biographies of the saints you learn that many became holy because they had suffered. For example, Saint Elizabeth Ann Seton lost her mother when she was only three years old. She later lost her sister, lost her husband in her twenties, and subsequently lost two of her children when she was a widow. She devoted her life to God and lived a holy life.

Saint Therese of Lisieux got sick when she was young and died at the age of twenty-four. She is one of the most popular saints.

I was in shock for three or four weeks from the time my son suddenly became sick and died. I coped with the pain, but I functioned minimally. I was not in denial, the first stage of loss, as Elizabeth Kubler-Ross discovered in her interviews with dying patients. I refer to Elizabeth Kubler-Ross's description of dying, because losing someone you deeply love is similar to dying. I was fully aware that Edward died, but it felt like a part of my anatomy was cut off. A part of me died inside, and my head was heavy. I was in a state of severe pain. I consciously used the mature ego defenses of altruism, suppression, anticipation, sublimation, and humor. I suffered a lot. Reflecting on Jesus Christ's suffering—His death and His resurrection—helped me heal myself. Rereading Buddha's teachings about getting rid of our attachments and rereading Taoism helped me, too.

It takes time to heal. It took me about four years to completely transcend and accept my sufferings as part of my lot in life. I also read some biographies, such as John Keats, Anne Frank, and Abraham Lincoln. I was particularly inspired by Abraham Lincoln's strength in turning his losses into constructive activities. He lost the only woman he ever loved, and lost one of his sons. He also had many failures in his career. He became one of our greatest presidents. During his presidency, he lost one more son.

My stages of grief were intense pain; a short period of depression where I wanted to sleep all the time; and later on, I accepted things. I did not exactly experience the typical stages of death and dying such as denial, anger, bargaining, depression and acceptance that Elizabeth Kubler-Ross wrote about in her book *On Death and Dying.*

Using sublimation, channeling my painful emotions into creative activities, I set up a library in one of the public schools in the Philippines in my son's memory six months after he died. I also decided to do something for him by writing this book. It makes me feel better to keep doing something constructive for his sake. I feel that the love that belongs to my son is permanent, and I am continuously thinking of ways to express my love for him. As the playwright Robert Anderson wrote, "Death ends a life, not a relationship."

Step by step, I became closer to God. Now I am able to offer my sufferings and my life for the glory of God. I developed more compassion, forgiveness, and empathy because I have suffered intensely. I am a better person because of it. I gained more virtues from my pain.

Adversity also helped me grow to become emotionally stronger. I am suffering the loss of my beloved son, but I am happy and have joy in my life. I achieved happiness and joy even if I lived with occasional pain by being emotionally mature and growing spiritually, that is, by loving everybody unconditionally. I am not always successful in doing so because some people are very difficult to love, but I try my best.

Pain, happiness, and joy can be experienced together. I am in pain but I am happy. Writing this book (sublimation) and my faith in God eased my pain gradually. I thank God that my pain is now almost gone. Healing is not a straight-line process. Some days I feel better than others. Each day I try using one or all of the five mature ego defenses until I feel better. I live with love, faith, courage, effort, and hope. I miss my son very much, but I am healed. This is one of the miracles in my life.

Pain
Endless pain
like endless rain.

Sometimes
the sun is hidden
by rain
as our love
is covered by pain.
Sometimes
strong pains
like heavy rain
destroy.

Endless pain
like endless rain
are invaluable—
pain brings us gain,
rain nourishes
living things.

Endless pain
like endless rain
makes us create
art and beauty.
It makes us see truth.

Eventually
we accept the pain
and the rain.

Reality
One penetrating truth
open our souls
like cracked coconuts—
We are no longer the same.

INDIVIDUATION

Individuation is knowing who we really are and living our truth. You accept and bear the life's pains and change what you can to better yourselves. It is not important what others think about you. What matters is that you love who and what you are.

There are three steps to individuation:

- Insight
- Endurance
- Action

Carl Gustav Jung created the term individuation to describe the process of acquiring self-knowledge, the way to describe one's true inner self and to have a truly integrated personality. It is the discovery of our total self, including the divinity in ourselves. We become childlike, authentic, and live our essence.

When you are lucky to spend time with preschool children, you will notice that they do things spontaneously and answer questions honestly. Adults are like that when they become individuated and childlike again. Jung focused on the second part of life as the start of individuation.

We rediscover ourselves through self-reflection as well as by being intimate with others. Each of us a unique individual. We have our individual histories—our triumphs and trials in life. Most of us are awakened by our pain. It makes us realize and deal with the reality of our human condition. Self-reflection, journaling, contemplation, and psychotherapy can make you aware of yourselves. Sometimes you realize that you are not living exactly as you want, that you are "living in the wrong shoes." So you change yourselves.

To change yourselves requires effort and courage. It is a manifestation of self-love.

Heidi was thirty-eight years old when she realized that she wanted to have a child. She saved her money for the next two years, and she was able to adopt an infant baby girl from Columbia. Her life became more complicated, and she had more problems to solve, but she was happy.

Your insights are useful for your growth. Once you have more insights, you endure your pain, suffering, sadness, and losses. You change to be better and more authentic persons. You change what you can and accept what you cannot.

Raymond realized at fifty that he wants to be a primary care physician. He endured the pain in his life and accepted that he was too old to go into medical school. Three years later, he took action and changed his life closer to his dream by doing some volunteer work at a hospice center.

As we grow, we become emotionally stronger, more loving, understanding, and accepting of our human condition. This takes time and work. It is not a quick fix. Unless we develop a cognitive disorder, we will continue to grow intellectually, emotionally, and spiritually until we die. As we age, our body continuously fails, but our intellectual or spiritual growth continues.

Maria came from Cuba thirty years ago. She lost her immediate family in Cuba. She worked as a cleaning woman and a sales clerk at a Spanish grocery store. She enrolled in a community college and learned English as a second language. Ten years ago, she became a teacher's aide and now goes to college to become a bilingual teacher. She had been very active in her church and had been a devoted Baptist. From reading the Bible and studying other religion, she changed and became a Catholic. Her friends were upset about her changing her religion, but she did it anyway and felt she was being true to herself. She is a cheerful person, and you would never know that she had a difficult life. When I am with her, I feel I can be myself because she is sincere and comfortable with herself, too. She is individuated, spiritual, and true to her core. I enjoy the time I spend with her.

Many people have good insights about their history, about what bothers them, and how they feel about things. But they don't do anything to change themselves and improve. They become stuck with their negative emotions and become chronically depressed. They are unable to grieve and move on.

To change and to grow takes a lot of energy and endurance. It takes energy and endurance to develop character. It is good to realize that the work we exert to grow is all worth it—a way to improve ourselves.

I know many people who have good insights, usually through psychotherapy, but who do not want to endure the pain and work that goes with changing themselves. They become chronically depressed and blame their circumstances for their miseries. They blame their miseries on other people that they believe are responsible for ruining their lives.

Others live in pain, and rather than sublimate their pain and express it creatively, they use drugs and alcohol to medicate their pain. They become self-destructive.

Wise action propels us into our new life. We can become more spiritual. Each day we can put our minds and hearts into what God wants us to do with our life. We can do God's will and can make this world better by doing even small things each day.

Clarisa is an example. She owns and is responsible for her life and lives the way she wants to live. She knows the good and bad things about her personality and accepts herself fully. Every day she does things to improve herself. She carries a to-do list every day. As soon as she wakes up, she says her prayers, does her housework, and does aerobic exercise for fifteen or twenty minutes. Then she cooks her family's meals and goes to work. When she comes home, she goes to her daughter's house to babysit for three hours. She is content with her life and solves her problems, whatever comes along. She does not envy nor wish her life could be different.

PEACE AND JOY

I achieved peace and joy in myself through my communion with God. Peace and joy are within me, and I feel it in my soul. Before my tragic loss, I achieved peace and joy when I meditated and was able to transcend outward things that bothered me. As I grow spiritually, peace and joy have become part of what I am all the time. It is my essence, and I carry it with me always. I do not carry grudges, fear, anger, envy, or other destructive emotions. I have these feelings every now and then, but I am able to let go of them. I am able to accept pain and suffering as part of my life.

Joy comes hand in hand with peace. It is God's gift to us. It is a by-product of our spirituality. When we live a good life, trust God with our lives, and do God's will, we feel joy in our hearts regardless of the problems we encounter from day to day. Each day becomes a gift—to give and to serve others.

Intelligence and formal education have no correlation with peace and Joy. I noticed that mentally challenged people live with peace and joy just like some intelligent and professional people do.

I have a patient who has Down syndrome. I saw her crying because of earaches, but she always exuded joy and peace in her eyes. She concentrated on feeling better and never complained about her misfortunes. Joy was God's grace given to her. I also have a patient with borderline IQ. She was joyful all the time whenever I saw her in the office.

Peace and joy is living fully in the present moment. Do not waste time thinking about the past, which can never be changed. Also, do not spend time worrying about the future. Use your energy in what is the best thing to do now.

You also achieve peace when you get rid of your pride and prejudice. Humility and acceptance of other people's differences can improve tolerance for people. Much of what bothers you about people is liable to be due to prejudice. When you are able to respect all people and tolerate and accept their idiosyncrasies, you live with more peace.

I try my best to give unconditional love to everybody with whom I interact. If someone does something bad to me, I try to forgive the person. I think of forgiveness, I feel forgiveness, and I act in a forgiving way by being good to the person who is being unkind to me. I am not always successful in doing this, but I spend time correcting myself to become more loving. Difficult acts take practice and patience.

Terry brought her friend with her to my office. It was the first time I met her friend. All of a sudden, Terry's friend said that they should get a lawyer and sue me for not diagnosing and treating my patients correctly. I really did not know what she was talking about. Instead of being upset and angry, I was calm and listened to her accusations.

Later on, I talked to God and asked Him for help and guidance. I carry a small notebook in which to write my daily goals in life as well as my positive affirmations and visualizations for thinking and doing constructive things. Prayers, especially silent or contemplative, and meditation always bring me peace and joy. I meditate on Jesus Christ's life when I say the rosary.

I do not always remember to be positive or proactive. Sometimes I act reactively, especially when I am busy and in a hurry. But I have learned not to say anything until I am able to review my affirmations and visualizations, and contemplate the presence of God within me, and of God within everyone. The prayer of Saint Francis of Assisi, which I included in Appendix B, is also a good prayer for achieving peace. His prayer is a guidepost in my daily life.

CHAPTER 3

— ❧ —

Self-Development

We can grow continuously from birth to old age.
There are many stages of our development from
birth to old age. We normally continue to grow
intellectually, emotionally, and spiritually as long
as our brain is functioning. The eight stages of
Eric Erickson's psychosocial life cycle stages of
development, self-love and self-esteem lead us to
have more capacity to have courage, hope, work,
understanding, play, and happiness. These are
part of the seventeen skill sets I recommend that
you use to have an authentically successful life.

PSYCHOSOCIAL LIFE CYCLE STAGES OF DEVELOPMENT

ERIC H. ERICKSON, winner of both the Pulitzer Prize and
National Book Award, and a professor of human development
at Harvard, wrote *Identity and The Life Cycle,*which describes
the eight major stages of psychosocial and developmental crises
from birth to maturity. Because of these crises, we develop
chronological and psychosocial strengths.

Here are the eight stages: excerpts taken from the above
mentioned book.

1. Infancy—Trust vs Mistrust
2. Early childhood—Autonomy vs Shame and Doubt
3. Play age—Initiative vs Guilt

4. School age—Industry vs Inferiority
5. Adolescence—Identity vs Identity Diffusion
6. Young Adult—Intimacy vs Isolation
7. Adulthood—Generativity vs Self-absorption
8. Mature age—Integrity vs Despair and Disgust

These developmental stages and characteristics are critical in successfully navigating our lives. You need to go through psychosocial crises and acquire strengths in every stage of your development from infancy to old age. If you do not successfully acquire these valuable chronological attributes during any of these stages, you need to develop them later on in life. Otherwise, you are handicapped by "unfinished business" in your journey to the next stages.

Christian grew up without developing autonomy. He was emotionally and financially dependent on his parents. He lacked confidence, had self-doubts and never learned to make decisions on his own. At twenty-five years old, he still lived with his parents. He dropped out of high school and stayed home and played video games practically all day long. His mother brought him to a psychiatrist at the insistence of his primary physician. He was diagnosed as having depression and is being seen by a psychotherapist besides his psychiatrist.

Nora grew up in a dysfunctional family. Her parents never spent time with her. When she was nineteen years old, she still had not learned how to be intimate. She kept her thoughts to herself. She got married at twenty, but never learned how to communicate and share her thoughts and feelings with her husband. After her divorce, she went from one dysfunctional relationship to another. At thirty years old, she read one of Eric Erickson's books out of serendipity and learned the developmental psychosocial stages. She changed herself and learned to be intimate with her friends. At forty years old, she found the love of her life, and now, ten years later, she is still happily married.

When you mature, your life focuses on giving. You achieve the stage of *generativity*. Nevertheless, some people get stuck and never grow up to be generative.

Arles is fifty years old and has only one friend, whom he has not seen for three years. He spends most of his time watching television, self-absorbed and self-centered. He is physically and financially capable to help others, but he is not doing any volunteer or altruistic things. He is unhappy and complains all the time. He has no desire to change himself and his lifestyle even though he lives in despair.

It is good to reflect periodically on your lives and change what you can in order to develop to your fullest potential; to make the best of whatever situations you are in. You can live with integrity. You do not want to be on your deathbed and realize that you have failed in life and lived in despair; that you made so many mistakes, or you wished that you could have lived differently, but you do not have any more time, effort, or courage to change yourselves and your path. It is good to reflect on your journey and say to yourselves, "I made lemonade out of lemons, and I can still better my life."

You can improve the quality of your journey as long as you live. Around the end of each year, I spend time just thinking about my life and deciding what to do next. It is good to decide what to get rid of in our lives and what bridges to cross at the present moment and into the future.

Esther considered herself a late bloomer. At age forty-five, after raising two successful children, she went back to school, took up architecture—an unusual and difficult career to start in older age—and became successful at her new career at age fifty-five. She chaired a nonprofit organization that helps people return to the workforce after spending time at home raising children. She had intimate friends, worked five days a week, played tennis, and hiked with her family on weekends. She was true to herself and lived with integrity. At sixty-five years old, she died in a car accident. Although her family was distraught, they were happy to remember that their mother lived a life that she had loved.

The Bug
Someone suddenly saw you jumping
and in a split second
you dropped
to the floor.

You came with the pink
lollipop poeny
I picked on my way
and carried with me
to the hospital
to give me
the experience
of what could happen.
In a second,
We can experience
what change and luck
can do to things;
what power nature has,
how things
can be beyond nature.

In seconds
the brain
can either live
or die;
in a second
our world
means something
or nothing at all.

SELF-LOVE AND SELF-ESTEEM

Self-love is a prerequisite to loving others. Hillel wrote, "If
you are not for you, who will be? If you are only for you, what's
the purpose? If not now, when?"

Self-love and self-esteem go together. When you love yourselves, you value and feel good about yourselves. Self-esteem means valuing and respecting who and what you are. You can take the time to reflect in order to know and understand yourselves. You believe in yourselves; you can keep developing your self-knowledge as you live. You know what you want, what you do not want, and what you like and dislike in people and things.

You can also become aware of your sexuality and orientation. You can have an insight as to whether you are gay, lesbian, bisexual, heterosexual, or asexual. You can then be honest with yourselves and seek relationships accordingly.

Uncommon sexuality was accepted even when I was still growing up in the Philippines, over fifty years ago. According to 2002 statistics from a young adult fertility and sexuality survey in the Philippines, 11 percent of sexually active Filipinos between ages fifteen and twenty-four have had sex with someone of the same sex. However, although same sex relationships in the Philippines have been socially accepted for generations, currently, same sex marriage is still not legally permitted. Currently, I accept whatever is a person's sexuality. It is tragic to live a life that is dishonest to yourself. You need to live with integrity, to always be true and follow what is in your heart.

Self-esteem is part of your self-development; it means living as an expression of your own truth. Once you become emotionally mature, self-esteem depends on your true selves, not what others think about you. You acknowledge the story of your life. You do not have to be ashamed of what you lack or of your mistakes or your deficiencies. Mistakes and deficiencies are part of your humanity.

Our life, whatever it may be, can be fine. We must accept our imperfections. The shining sun and the colorless rain—both can make us bloom. We live fully each day and solve our problems as they come, the best way we can. We respect people around us but do not depend on them for our self-esteem. Again, our self-esteem depends on ourselves. We live as we are.

Cora is a housewife who volunteers at the Red Cross and the soup kitchen for the homeless. She also cooks and brings food to several people who need nutritious meals. She is doing what she wants to do with her life, and she likes herself. She has strong self-esteem and is not interested in a high-powered career or doing things to follow her mother's dreams for her. Cora is a retired first grade teacher who graduated summa cum laude from Princeton University. Her mother wanted her to be a medical doctor or a physicist since she was very good in science. She did not follow her mother's dream for her; she is doing what she wants to do with her life.

When we do not feel good about ourselves, we can repeat positive affirmations, such as "I love myself unconditionally." When I have a difficult day, I say to myself, "It is not really so bad." I concentrate on this thought, and after a few minutes I feel better. When I make a mistake, I correct myself and tell myself, "I will do better next time."

You can visualize yourselves as happy persons doing the best that you are able to do. You can keep doing constructive things for yourselves and for others. Doing something good can makes you feel good. Enhancing other people's self-esteem can enhance your own self-esteem. You can enhance people's self-esteem by valuing them. When you accept who they are, you can make them feel good about themselves by sincerely appreciating and validating what you like about them. You are courteous toward them. You are not critical about what you dislike about them. You encourage what is good in people while overlooking and accepting their imperfections.

Find something good in people and bring out the best in them. Appreciate, approve, and accept what you can. Doing this can enhance your self-esteem as well as theirs. The book *Course in Miracles* says that what we give, we simultaneously receive. If you see what is wrong and undesirable in others, you can give constructive suggestions when appropriate.

Motivate yourself to do things for others. It is never too late to change in a positive way. It is not constructive to find excuses for those things for which you are responsible. You have to learn and use common sense. You can become wise and apply what you have learned as you are living.

If you had parents who validated your true self while you were growing up, you were fortunate. Singer Jennifer Hudson exudes self-confidence and credits her mother for giving her a lot of support, validation, and confidence while she was growing up. Self-esteem is the strength that makes us realize our dreams and potential.

My daughter, Melin, is a confident person. She is a successful and accomplished otolaryngologist, with a subspecialty in microscopic laryngology. She also spends time supporting her community. Growing up, I supported her whatever she wanted to be and do.

If you were not so fortunate, you can be your own nurturing parent. It may then be harder to acquire the courage to be who and what you are, but you can still do it.

Cultivating cheerfulness can also increase self-esteem. See the bright side of things as much as possible. There is a silver lining in every dark cloud. Watch the movie *Pollyanna,* a 1960 Walt Disney film, or read the classic 1913 children's book *Pollyanna* by Eleanor H. Porter. The word *Pollyanna* is now used as a noun to describe a person characterized by irrepressible optimism and a tendency to find good in any situation. Some people use the adjective *Pollyannaish* with a negative connotation of being optimistic to a fault. Just remember the word *Pollyanna* as a constructive description of being optimistic in life.

To live with high self-esteem, you have to be emotionally self-reliant. You do not depend solely on others for your happiness and fulfillment of your needs. Yet, we are all part of this one world. Any changes in the world affect us, like the famous *butterfly effect*, which teaches that sometimes a small action can lead to enormous consequences globally. We are interdependent. In chaos theory, the butterfly effect is the dependence on initial conditions, where a small change in one place can result in large difference to a later state. The name of the effect is coined by Edward Lorenz, derived from a theoretical example of a hurricane formation dependent on whether or not a butterfly had flapped its wings many weeks before.

In order to be successfully interdependent, you must first develop your own independence or self-reliance. You live healthier lives if you give to the world—if you give to enhance your relationships. President John F. Kennedy, in his inaugural speech said, "And so, my fellow Americans: ask not what your country can do for you—ask what you can do for your country. My fellow citizens of the world: ask not what America will do for you, but what together we can do for the freedom of man … here on earth God's work must truly be our own."

Arrival
You express
who and what you are
like the bright blue bell
that smiles in the rain.
Your eyes cannot deceive
even those who never
understand why.

Truth, when lived,
means that your soul
lights your torch
and shows the world
that you have arrived.

Notice these people
Those who have strong
Self-esteem
believe in themselves.

They know themselves—
what they want.
They are living
the life they love—
the best they can create.

They are disciplined
and follow
their bliss.

COURAGE

The stronger our faith in God, the stronger our courage. One of my favorite songs is by David Haas, with lyrics quoted from the Bible: "Do not be afraid; I am with you." It takes courage to live and keep on going even when life is complicated, painful, and difficult. I always remind myself of inspiring stories about people who have continued to have the courage to live worthwhile, even exceptional lives, despite their tragic and traumatic experiences. These include such notable figures as Viktor Frankl, Oprah Winfrey, Zheng Cao, Tony Meléndez, and Gabrielle Gifford.

Viktor Frankl was a psychiatrist who spent three years in a concentration camp. His parents and wife were killed in a gas chamber; yet he found meaning in his suffering and wrote his famous book, *Man's Search for Meaning*. He became the father of logotherapy.

Oprah Winfrey is a self-made billionaire who had a difficult childhood. She wrote, "I have a lot of things to prove to myself. One is that I can live my life fearlessly." Part of her life is devoted to helping millions of people improve their lives.

Zheng Cao is an opera singer. She never smoked, yet was diagnosed with incurable stage four lung cancer. She underwent chemotherapy and radiation and continues to sing. I have chills when I listen to her sing "Over the Rainbow."

Tony Meléndez was born in Nicaragua. He was born without arms because his mother took an antinausea pill while pregnant. He is a "thalidomide person." He sings while playing a guitar with his feet. Pope John Paul II was so moved when he heard him play in 1978 in Los Angeles that he kissed him. Meléndez practices his music six to seven hours every day. He has been touring the United States and is an inspiration to thousands of people.

Congresswoman Gabrielle Gifford's husband assured the nation in January 2011 that his wife has an indomitable spirit and sense of humor. She had started to recover well and started to speak after the brain surgery needed because of a gunshot wound. On April 27, 2011, she was televised walking by herself to board a helicopter to watch her husband take off in a space shuttle. She touched her colleagues and many people watching the news when she appeared in Congress to vote yes to support a bill to raise our national debt in order to help balance our country's budget.

It takes courage to be true to ourselves and live as an expression of who and what we are. We have to own our lives and be accountable for our choices. It takes courage to really live, not just exist. I try not to waste my time and energy on destructive and unimportant things. I make a point to evaluate my day before I sleep. I write in my journal the things I can do to improve the quality of my life the following day. Frequently, I ask myself: "Am I doing what makes me healthy and happy? Am I spending my time doing what is important to me? How can I love better? Am I walking on the right path?" I believe that love or God is the answer for everything. I try to practice compassion and forgiveness with myself and the people with whom I interact from day to day. I remind myself of a friend's advice: "Love unconditionally."

Sacrifice and the acceptance of suffering are virtues. I am not always successful, but I try my best each day. I also make it a point to try to overcome my fears. I am afraid to ride on an airplane, but I do it anyway. I used to be nervous speaking in public because I had not done it during my school years. I overcame that fear by practicing at a Toastmasters Club. We become good at what we want to do by practice, practice, and more practice.

People develop courage by doing things that they are afraid to do. You need to take risks in life. It takes courage to love. It takes courage to confront those you love, share your opinion, and tell them that what they are doing is not constructive to themselves or to others. It takes courage to make a commitment and to assert independence from parents and other significant relationships. People develop courage one step at a time. You build your muscles when you keep on using them. The more you exercise your courage, the more courageous you become.

I was delighted to see my five-year-old grandson Zachary play the cello for his friend who came to visit after school. I remember when I was ten years old. I was timid and would cry if my mother asked me to play the piano for visitors. I was also impressed when my two-year-old grandson took swimming lessons. I considered him to be courageous because I have seen other children, even the older ones, who were afraid to swim.

Courage (One)
To commit
to love
a life partner
is to risk
being hurt.

To laugh
is to risk
being mistaken
as a fool.

To be true
is to risk
being labeled
stupid.

To play
is to risk
losing.

But
not to have
the courage
to be
is not
to live.

Courage (Two)
It takes courage
to love
to live
to suffer
to grow
to grow old
to die.

Reality of our human condition
We go through legitimate pain
in our lives; we experience
legitimate suffering
no matter who, what, and where we are.

Pain and suffering
do not take away
our ability to love life;
we can have a happy, loving,
fulfilled—
a magnificent life
despite pain and suffering
sometimes because
of them. We value
and use each moment
of our lives productively
because we know
that we will die;

not me alone
not you alone
but each and every one
of us.

We can live
a life that's unforgettable
in a very short time
or we can live
a life that's unremarkable
in numerous years.

We co-create
our life
with God
and find our own answers;
we know
when we have the right answers
for our heart like the magnificent star knows
when we are living with our essence.

Illness
When we are ill,
we want to scream;
we want to run away;
far,
far,
far away;
hoping
our illness will be left behind;
so then....
we will be well,
we will be well!

After some time
we begin
to think sharply,
we see ourselves clearly
as a single flower wilting!

We are most aware,
most focused
when we are conscious
there is death
and we can die!

.... then,
we resolve,
we do not want to die!
we will do everything
to make ourselves well!
we do not want
those we love
to be hurt,
to be left by themselves
without our assistance,
our human love,
our physical presence,
our laughter!

HOPE

When we are hopeful or optimistic, difficult things become a little easier to do. When you are confronted with painful losses, you can hope for a better future ahead. You can say to yourselves that these trying times will pass. When you are ill but believe that you will get better, often your health improves. I write positive affirmations and read them as daily reminders. Some of my affirmations are:

Personal:

- I am healthy.
- I am happy.
- I have a lot of energy.
- I commune with God the Father, God the Son, and God the Holy Spirit.

- I have peace, joy, and love.
- I live with discipline.
- I am doing what is good.

Life:

- I am going to make today the best day of my life.
- Today is a good day.
- It is good to persevere and keep trying.
- I can do all good things with God's help.

We can also do visualization. I incorporate my feelings when I visualize. We can visualize our affirmations and also experience the feelings generated from our affirmations and visualizations.

I love the seas, the skies, and the stars. I feel the love I have while I imagine the beauty of nature. I sometimes visualize myself sitting by the blue ocean on the white sand—so happy—and later on, walking on the boardwalk, singing. These calming scenes relax me and restore my energy. Visualizing my time spent with my two grandchildren makes me so happy. When I am sad about something, I visualize the things we do together, and it brings me gratitude and joy. I frequently visualize our walks to the park, the laughter, and the times on the swing; the time when Zachary and I went to the toy store and he asked me, "Did you bring some money, Grandma?" Then he said, "There is nothing like going to the toy store." I also visualize Emmett swimming by himself and then looking at me with a smile on his face.

You can write your own affirmations and practice visualizations with your emotions. Change them as the need arises. In life, you need to persevere and persist in doing things in order to be successful in accomplishing your goals. You are more motivated to persist and persevere when you believe that someday you can accomplish the goals you are striving to achieve.

Another thing you can do is to anchor relaxing and happy visualizations to your fingers. By touching a finger where you anchored your feelings, you will experience the anchored feelings immediately.

Matthew anchored his relaxing feelings and visualization on his third finger. Whenever he experienced some tenseness in his neck muscles, he touched his third finger and felt relaxed.

One of my patients is physically, intellectually, emotionally, and spiritually healthy. He got that way by living with tremendous hope in his life. He told me that his hope for a better life made him healthy, and he became a well-respected teacher in his town. He was the first person in his family to go to college. He was a working student. And there were semesters when he was not able to go to school, but he persevered and eventually realized his dream.

People with high levels of hope do not give in easily to severe anxiety, discouragement, difficult challenges, or setbacks. In the wake of such trials, they can experience less anxiety, depression, and emotional distress. Psychologist Martin Seligman, at the University of Pennsylvania, found that new salesmen who were optimistic sold 37 percent more insurance during the first two years on their job as compared to pessimists. Daniel Goleman, in his famous book *Emotional Intelligence*, wrote, "Optimism and hope, like helplessness and despair, can be learned. Underlying both is an outlook psychologists call self-efficacy: The belief that one has mastery over events of one's life and can meet challenges as they come up."

My mother told us, "Where there is life, there is hope." I acquired my medical degree, finished the required postgraduate examinations in the Philippines, and started working as a medical intern here in the United States at age twenty-four, after a year of volunteer work as a rural general physician at home. Although our education in the Philippines was in English, I studied Chinese, and Filipino (Tagalog) as well. Our island has a local dialect that we spoke apart from Tagalog (our national language). I went to school without reading any textbooks until I was in my third year of medical school. Subsequently, I had difficulties expressing myself and taking essay tests. In our third year, we were required to write histories, physical examinations, and answers in essay form.

My daughter had a different medical curriculum here in the US. She wrote histories and physical examinations starting in her first year. I remember being unable to describe "pros and cons" because I did not know what the question meant. I failed a clinical subject and had to repeat my fourth year of medical school. That year I learned to read textbooks and prepared for the English language exam to come to America as an exchange student. I passed the medical and English exams required to work here as a medical intern before I graduated medical school.

I took up writing only within the past fifteen years. My son taught me how to write my first poem. Writing together is one of my fondest memories of him. Growing up, I imitated my mother, who played the piano by ear. I studied piano for two years in grade school and found it to be very difficult. My piano teacher used to stay in her kitchen cooking a meal, and she would shout at me, "Wrong notes!" My daughter taught me classical piano for five years, and I found it to be relatively easy. She made piano lessons fun. It was hope that made me continue to work and persevere with my dreams.

This is a poem that my son and I wrote together. He said, "Let me show you, Mom."

Piano lessons

We bought our first piano (I was eight)
at the World's Fair in Manila,
where Armi Kussella was crowned Miss Universe,
her beaded dress emitting sparks of light.
Trailing scents of jackfruit, mango,
Calamine, and mentholate,
my mother led me through streets pressed
in arms and legs, her aroma mingling

with still heavier air:
fried bananas, peanuts roasting
laced with honey, cinnamon curry,
jasmine anisette-
a tropical slipstream in which I breathed
content, these fragrances a veil
to cloak me from
the darkest night.

The second piano that I bought
was for my children,
the sort of gift they might improve upon in time,
by mastering the lessons as I had not,
allowing school lectures and medical studies,
an early marriage, a later divorce,
to keep me from
the thing I loved.
Only later, a half century later,
with my children out of the house and two dogs in
their place,
have I returned to taking lessons,
this time from my daughter
clapping hands and tapping feet
to chide me through
uncertain notes and beats.

Struggling this time
with the teacher I have raised,
to learn the lessons she has mastered,
we spend as many moments laughing
as enduring the other's diligence,
reliving all the years in between
parsed in syncopated breaths.
And I sense now as we sit down
to the third piano that I bought,
neither for my children nor my living room, but for
myself;
a rush of memory luminous in lacquer black,
of languid air, of jungle night

and lingering above them all remembered
music from the farther room
half a world away.

In mythology, Pandora, a princess of ancient Greece, was
given a mysterious box by the gods who were jealous of her
beauty. Pandora lifted the lid of the box to see what was inside.
Disease, malady, and madness came out; but a merciful god let
her close the box just in time for hope to remain inside, the one
antidote that makes life's misery bearable.

Dew
Few drops of dew
on the bright red hibiscus.
Few drops of hope
in our heart.
Why only a few drops of dew?
Why not a sea, a river?
Why only a few drops of hope?
Why not big dreams to come true?
Hope is the tiny flame
that makes us live,
is a ray from the sunshine
that nurtures who we are,
is the thread that stitches us
into what we are,
is the will
and the way
that makes our dreams
come true.

WORK

Part of being mentally healthy is doing meaningful work.
We have to engage in fulfilling work, something that uses
our talents and energy. One antidote for a depressed mood is

work. We can channel our disturbing and painful emotions into constructive work.

Leo Tolstoy kept writing in spite of feeling depressed while living a miserable family life. His art helped him cope with his circumstances. Beethoven was almost completely deaf when he composed his ninth symphony. Carl Jung wrote his greatest work when he was in his eighties. He died at age eighty-six. Norman Vincent Peale kept an active work life almost all of his life. He died at age ninety-five.

I encourage my patients who retire from their jobs to try doing different things that will fulfill them. Some people who worked for decades to earn a living never had the privilege of working at a career they love. I tell them, "Now that you are retired, it is your chance to do what you really love." There is always something one can do, perhaps volunteer work, helping someone in other ways, or doing creative things.

Periodically, I see patients who complain that they cannot find something that they want to do. I tell them, "Do something; any creative activity will do. Pretend to enjoy it, and eventually you might actually enjoy doing it." Often on their next visit, with smiles on their faces, they report that my suggestion had worked.

M. Scott Peck, MD, in his best-selling book *The Road Less Traveled,* defined love as "the will to extend oneself for the purpose of nurturing one's own or another's spiritual or intellectual growth." He made no distinction between spiritual and intellectual growth. Loving requires effort and courage. Leo Tolstoy wrote, "One can live magnificently in this world if one can work and love. To work for the one you love and to love one's work." Sigmund Freud, a neurologist at the turn of the twentieth century, defined mental health as the ability to love and to work: *Leibe und arbeit, arbeit und leibe, das ist alles ist.* (Love and work, work and love, that's all there is.)

Time is limited, so spend it wisely. One good question to ask yourself periodically is: "If I were going to die in six months, am I spending my time the way I want to right now?" I have a bucket list, and I refer to it when I am making my schedule. Now that I am seventy-two, I have learned to live for the day. I make each day the best day of my life. I have become more focused and spend my time in what I really want to do. I enjoy every dawn, regardless of the weather. I enjoy each day as it moves toward the night. Douglas Pagels wrote, "A life well lived is simply a compilation of days well spent." I have accepted my misfortunes, pains, and hardship; and live with gratitude for my blessings.

Other important activities are physical and mental exercises. I do my physical exercises right after I wake up. I am a morning person. It is easier for me to do difficult things in the morning. I do not ask myself whether I feel like doing them, I just do them.

A patient asked me, "Do you like to exercise?"

I told her, "Sometimes I do not feel like doing it, but I do it anyway because it's good for me. Physical exercise gives me more energy. It gives me a sense of well-being throughout the day, helps me to cope with stress, and to develop self-esteem and self-mastery. And it helps me spend a worthwhile day."

Physical exercise is an antidote to feeling tired. When you do not engage in any strenuous physical activities all day and feel you have no energy to exercise, that is when you should really make the time to exercise. Walking at least six miles per week regenerates nerve cells, improves memory, and delays the onset of Alzheimer's disease (NIH—National Institute on Aging, 2013).

Mental exercises, such as studying, learning a musical instrument, writing, and teaching are worthwhile activities that also prolong the onset of memory loss and senile dementia

Having a healthy mind and body are worth all our efforts. We can vary the type of exercises that we do. Statistics show that it takes twenty-one days to make exercise a habit, and it takes six months to make it become a way of life. It is good to remember not to quit exercising if possible, because once we stop it is harder to start again.

Recently, I developed degenerative arthritis in my left knee. I still exercise using a DVD; you can work out sitting down.

Work
Work is love
and love is work.
It is both sides of a coin—
they go together.

An endless day in ICU
How are you?
What are you thinking?
I should not have asked
since your face
and tone of voice
expressed
anger and pain.

I should have asked myself instead,
how can we transcend
the hurt and pain
in the nerve endings
of your body?

The resting soul
will wake up
and heal the hurt and the pain
as the sun rises
to light the earth
and brighten the world;
as the winds like Brahms' lullaby
comfort the leaves;
as a single flower blooms
to give you strength and hope.

It is not a question of why,
it is rather the acceptance
of what is
and responding with love.

It is when we know pain
very well that we appreciate
many other things more.
When we know pain
very well
it awakens us to life.

My Cave
Where I write
is a room without windows.
I do not see anything
besides a copying machine, a telephone,
two extra chairs, and a window-sized mirror.

When I write,
I do not want to be under the shining sun,
the bursting orchard's blossoms,
wind's whispers or the sounds of seas.
These are things I enjoy, but they don't help me write.

When I write
there is no set time. I do not follow
the circadian rhythm, the movements of the moon
or the schedule of my dog;
I depend on how clear my mind is
and whether I can hear the half-forgotten,
half-dream work of my imagination.

Where I write
my heart empties memories
and dreams are many dreams
that do not die.

Faces
Most days
I see many faces.
I look at them
like a botanist
looking closely

at a single flower
while the sun
looks at a single leaf.

Life and time
change our faces
like the caterpillars
becoming butterflies,
like the sweet wild camias
growing wilder.

We must live
each moment
fully
with open arms
as nothing,
nothing
stays
the same.

Prescriptions
Let the bees
have flowers.
Let the skies
have stars.
Let ourselves
have each other.
Let ourselves
be
love.

My Patient/Friend
I was not ready
when your heart stopped
like I was not wearing
a raincoat when it rained.

I was also not ready
to talk about you

when it was time
to share memories
of you.
My heart felt the familiar feelings
of loss,
my thoughts concentrated
on what could have been done differently.
I listened to your best friend,
the minister, others
who spoke what they knew about you.
I was in awe of hearing
what you'd accomplished—
things you had never talked about.
One of your friends blurted out,
"She did not brag about things."

I first met you
thirty-six years ago, the same
year I started my practice in Elizabeth.
How fortunate that I was your
physician ever since.
You were independent, intelligent, sincere,
appreciative, and direct.
You enjoyed church, people, choir,
running rummage sales, and sports.
You possessed a terrific sense of humor;
you were the first to laugh
at yourself. With a laughter
I can still hear,
you've repeatedly said "You see, I can eat but I cannot
taste, and Alice, your co-teacher, can taste but
cannot eat."

I saw you in my office, at the hospitals,
at your home by the lake, at your apartment,
and at the nursing home.
You knew and lived
what was important in life.
You were a role model for

living with our essence, giving,
being in touch with our feelings, sharing,
living the best we can.

You have lived and loved.
You have left a legacy.
You have made a difference to others
and in my life. You are in my heart.

UNDERSTANDING

Our capacity to understand ourselves, people, and things can help us adapt to life successfully. It is useful to read and study, to reflect, and to learn more in order to know more and understand better. As long as we are living, we have to keep learning.

We often get rid of our anger when we understand a situation better. One of the seven habits of highly effective people as written by Steven Covey is "Seek first to understand, then to be understood," just like in the prayer of St. Francis of Assisi. (See Appendix B.)

We need to learn how to communicate effectively. President Ronald Reagan said that a lot of the problems in the world would disappear if people would start talking *to* each other instead of talking *about* each other. We should practice learning how to listen well. We should listen well and concentrate on what other persons are trying to communicate to us instead of concentrating while that person is still talking on what we want to say. After we understand the person who is speaking, we can share our life and our ideas sincerely, in order to be understood.

It is beneficial to develop true friends with whom we can share our life, our ideas, and our opinions. We can cultivate friendships with trustworthy people. The resources we have available to learn, share, and communicate are expanding tremendously. With the Internet, we can search for information; we can easily ask questions to friends and people all over the world who have the expertise we hope to acquire.

No two people are the same. We need to respect other people's way of seeing and doing things. We can strive to understand rather than to be understood. (Again, see the prayer of Saint Francis of Assisi in Appendix B.) As we grow in experience and learning, we understand more but remain limited, so we have to make allowances for our limitations as well as those of others.

Good communication is also essential for good parenting. We teach our children effectively and boost their self-esteem when we talk with them and explain things at their level. We can become wiser in life by learning to understand things. My grandson Emmett Edward, at age two, kept asking Why? He was very curious. Every time he was told something, he would say Why? Other children I knew at age two, did not ask Why? as often as Emmett did.

We can learn what motivates us to do things. In general, we are motivated by love, sexual desire, anger, and fear; the need for financial security, self-preservation, freedom of body and mind; the desire for recognition and self-expression; and the goal of eternal life with God, for those who believe that there is life after death.

We can observe what goes on in the world and the people around us. We can learn the human condition and accept life's sufferings and the temporary aspect of existence. This knowledge helps us focus on what is really important and live from our essence.

I have been reading the Bible. First I read several children's Bibles covering the Old and New Testaments from cover to cover to learn the stories and understand the scriptures in simpler words. Now I am reading the New Revised American Standard Bible as well as other versions of the Bible, as they are written beautifully in various ways. Some words touch me more in one version than another. I also have my treasured large Holy Bible containing both the Old and New Testaments, which I bought at a garage sale while looking for children's books to donate to the Philippines.

One theory is that our brains have conscious, subconscious, and unconscious components. Some believe that our personal unconscious is connected to a universal consciousness or God-consciousness. We can draw wisdom from our unconscious through meditation and dreams. In Eastern meditation, we tap into wisdom through silencing our conscious thoughts and being present with our heart, which is connected to our unconscious and universal- or God-consciousness. As Jung wrote, our dreams reveal solutions to conflicts within our psyche. In *Dreams: The Collected Works of C. G. Jung,* he discussed the role of our unconscious in helping us resolve our psychic problems.

In 1890, the German Chemical Society organized an elaborate appreciation in honor of August Kekulé, celebrating the twenty-fifty anniversary of his first paper on benzene. On that occasion Kekulé said that he discovered the ring shape of the benzene molecule after having a daydream of a snake seizing his own tail—his story of the discovery of the benzene ring.

In the Old Testament, there are many stories about using dreams to predict the future. Many Bible stories are about dreams that came true as interpreted by wise people. At times, someone tells us something and we intuitively know it to be true. If we believe in God, this is God's gift to us coming from our unconscious. I believe that God is operative in our lives.

There are many ways of understanding and interpreting life. My girlfriend strongly believes in destiny. I believe that there are no accidents in life. Life is like the song "Que Sera, Sera," made popular by Doris Day. The lyrics say: "Whatever will be, will be; the future's not ours to see."

We can establish our own philosophy of life. During his high school days, my son loved "To strive, to seek, to find, and not to yield," from the poem "Ulysses" by Alfred Lord Tennyson. We can know which things are really important to us and live our values. My own philosophy is to be my best; to live simply and live as a good and loving person. Follow the Golden Rule, I forget myself, and focus on giving to others. My best friend, who is my age, tells me, "Live today and this is all we have."

Stephen Covey, in his book, *The Seven Habits of Highly Effective People*, wrote, "Begin with the end in mind and put first things first." Hans Selye, MD, the "Father of stress," wrote in his classic book, *Stress without Distress* that his philosophy of earning his neighbor's love as best he could, had made his life a happy one.

Throughout our lifetime, we have to continue to learn new things. There are always new inventions, new trends, and new discoveries. The world changes; and we must constantly adapt, change, be flexible, and revise our world view as needed. There are many things that are beyond our ability to reason and understand. There are so many whys and so many questions that we are not capable of answering correctly or with certainty. Many things remain a mystery. I believe that God will reveal more things to us only after we die. Perfect knowledge and perfect truth are possessed only by God.

I have a friend who does not believe in God. I have asked him what he thinks about the questions in life to which we have no definite answers. He said, "I do not know, but just because I do not know does not mean that I should believe in God." He happens to be functioning well, and so far he is living a charmed life without needing God. I told him that even if he is doing well, believing in God will make his life much better and more peaceful. I told him stories of the saints and holy people, and gave him books about them and the joyful lives they lived. My intention was to add something for him to ponder. I told him, "You can take it or leave it." He said, "I feel in my heart that you are my good friend."

Progress
Ten years ago, when I visited my family in the Philippines,
they were not as curious about New York
as about the nursing homes in America.

It was common knowledge in the Philippines
that nurses were in demand here in the United States
because nursing homes
were as common as shopping malls.

In the city where my relatives lived
there were no nursing homes.
We had orphanages, homeless people living on the
streets,
beggars, extreme poverty
but no nursing homes.
We took care of our family at home until they died.
We revered and respected old people.
We gave up our comforts
and goals for our parents and relatives.

Last year, when I went back home,
many homes had cable televisions.
They knew more of what's shown on TV.
My family was surprised that I had not seen most TV
shows.

This year when I go home,
I am sure they will tell me what I do not know
about the world. There will be no more questions
about nursing homes and nurses' jobs. They know
we have a distinct eastern heritage. It is different from
what goes on here in America.
This is progress!

My Culture
I am a Filipina.
A name for a woman
Born in the Philippine Islands.

Filipinas and Filipinos are generally happy—
Born with a Pollyanna attitude,
Content,
Easy going—

The sea breeze surrounded us
When we were born,
Able to take an enormous
Amount of suffering
And misfortune.
When one is sick
Or suffers a disaster,
The whole clan,
The whole barrio
Gathers to help
And share the emotions.
When someone walks
Into a good fortune,
Many will feel entitled
To a share
Of the pie.

Filipinos and Filipinas
Have great respect
For parents
And elders.
We also feel
It is our duty
To take care of
And help our family.

Filipinas and Filipinos
Love music, dance, drama, and romance.
Native musical instruments
Are made of bamboo,
Coconut, and wood.
We have our own love songs
For many generations,
Ballads recited
Again and again.
We have our own dances
Choreographed
Imitating the rhythm of the storms.
Our stories and dramas

Are full of romance and love.
We learn our fairy tales early on.
At 24, I carried
My fairy tales
When I came here.

Filipinas and Filipinos
Are mostly practicing Catholics.
We also have Protestants, born-again Christians,
Buddhists and a minority of Muslims in the south.
We have countless shrines
And stories of God's miracles.
Many Catholics name their children
After the saints.
I was named
After the Blessed Virgin Mother's apparition in Spain,
"Nuestra Señora del Pilar."

We have native, Spanish, Chinese,
And a few American, Hindu, Australian, and various
European blood all over
The country.
I have native, Chinese, and Spanish blood myself.
Our ways of preparing foods, eating, entertaining,
Wearing clothes, communicating
Are based on our rich heritage.
We usually speak our national language—Tagalog,
And simple English.
Some speak Chinese, Spanish,
And many local dialects as well.

In the midst of poverty,
Our culture values
Money and power
More than health and love.
Unless you already
Have money and power
It is not uncommon
For people to think

That there is something
Really ill about you
For wanting
Something else.

When we live abroad-
Mostly in the United States, Saudi Arabia, Taiwan,
Hong Kong, Singapore, Canada;
And go back home,
We bring "balikbayan" boxes and boxes
Of "pasalubong."
Gifts are for our family—
Immediate and ten times removed,
For our friends,
For the friends of our friends,
For the friends of our friend's friends.

Prudence
The more we understand,
The more clearly we see things as clear as water.

The more careful we become,
We see shadows even on a cloudy day.

The more flexible we are,
We adapt easily like violets
Moving with the sun.

The Bible tells
Stories about the wisdom
Of prudence.
We can live running
Day and night
But it is prudent to walk
On the ground
Day by day.

Justice
In our temporary present existence

In general, there is no justice.
Life is not fair.

Laws are made and remade.
Issues are argued by the lawmakers,
Lawyers and judges;
To make things work,
To at least achieve fairness,
Prevent more crimes
And hopefully
Have peace and order.

We are our own judges
Of ourselves.
Our conscience
Knows what is right
And what is wrong.

PLAY

Play is a gift that we give to ourselves. It is rejuvenating. If we do not play, we become old quickly. Sigmund Freud wrote, "In life we have to work, love, and play." This formula is a tripod. If it is not balanced, then the tripod will not stand up well. You make time for yourselves to play. Enjoy our own company, and enjoy spending time playing with your friends. You can laugh often, play with the winds, and count the stars. Be like the children playing in the park. Make play a part of your daily life.

There are many benefits from playing. Sports help you experience teamwork, trust, losses, and victories; playing them helps you experience some realities, some truths about life. Playing together also allows you to build friendships and meaningful relationships.

We can learn self-discipline and how to obey rules through play. Accomplished musicians spend many hours playing their music. They learn to follow rules passed down through generations. They learn and experience the advantages of expressing their sublime feelings while playing their music.

The kind of play we do depends on where we live and what is happening in our lives. When I was growing up in the Philippines, we picked and bartered with wild flowers and leaves. We made dolls from cut-out newspaper pictures and houses from boxes. Sometimes I would go down to the creek and try to catch fish. After I caught one, I would put it in a jar filled with water to show my friends. We told imaginary stories and drew imaginary people made of clay on the ground. We also played hopscotch. My parents stopped us from playing only when it became dark. We did not have electricity and used kerosene lamps in certain parts of the house. My mother told me that when I was about three years old, I often asked her why the moon followed me everywhere whenever I was outside. I also said, "When I grow big, I will go to the moon and ask her why she was always following me."

My grandsons live in the city. At two-and-a-half years old, Emmett Edward learned about the stars, planets, and moon at the Museum of Natural History. On his way home, he noticed the moon, too. When he got inside their apartment, he asked, "Why did the moon stop following me inside?" Besides going to the playground to play with their friends, my grandsons consider trips to the museums as play, and they have play-dates spending time in the museum together.

When my own children were growing up, they played with many different kinds of toys. My grandchildren also play with a lot of toys, such as trucks, stuffed animals, musical instruments, Legos and trains. They play competitive sports, too. I think that, although my playthings differed from those of my children and grandchildren, we had the same fun experiences with different resources. Zachary brought a plaque from camp that read, "If you want to be helpful, play with your friends."

My children traveled a lot by themselves and with their friends, but I spent many memorable, learning, and fun vacations with my children too. We traveled together to Japan, the Philippines, England, Paris, the Scandinavian countries, Israel, and some parts on the East coast and in California.

Unfortunately, I did not learn how to play their board games, but they played among themselves. They used to have sleepover parties. They played hide-and-seek with our neighbors. They wore costumes on Halloween and went around the neighborhood after school until dark. We had a farm with a pond. Edward and Melin used to spend days swimming and catching fish. They had pet rabbits, fish, and turtles. Pingry School had a strong athletic curriculum. My children used to play team sports and track after class.

My son and I used to browse through books at Barnes and Noble every Saturday. We learned a lot together and had fun sharing what we found to be interesting and humorous. We went to concerts and Broadway plays, especially during the holiday season. When we came home, we had fun discussing our experiences.

These are some of my happy memories. I am sharing them because they are treasures I carry in my heart. They make me smile, and I revere about them whenever I feel sad.

Vacation in Israel
Sharing thoughts, feelings,
experiences with my two children.

Answering questions,
questioning my answers, sharing.

Sharing the beauty of sunrises,
sunrays, sunsets; colors
in light yellow chrysanthemums
to the darkest marigolds.
Sharing the moonlights, the deserts,
floating in the Dead Sea, swimming in the Mediterranean.

Sharing the walks to the museums, churches, side streets,
parks, the quarters of old Jerusalem.

Sharing the foods that taste spicy and fresh,
the atmosphere of laughter, adventure, fun, and awe.

Playing alone, playing together, sharing.
Being very close, knowing each other more, sharing.

Play is a good way to develop creativity. Here in America, people play a lot and are creative. Our country invented so many amazing things, such as Microsoft Windows, Apple computers, eBay, Facebook, songs, and Broadway plays. You can live in New York City and enjoy many, many forms of art. Other countries have their own movies and inventions, too. I recently saw a series of amazing foreign films shown at a local university.

We live and express our humanness by being able to play. Let us have a balanced life. We can do work, love, and play each day, each month, and each year of our lives.

HAPPINESS

Everyone wants to be happy. There are temporary things that make us happy. We have individual desires that influence our happiness from day to day. From time to time we experience situations and problems. If these are changed for the better or we overcome our problems, we become happy. If we have money problems and solve them by getting a well-paying job, then we are happy when we get the job. Happiness is like grapes. The deeper part is more valuable and tastes better than the skin or the surface.

When we become emotionally mature, our values change, and we find other things that make us happy. In his book *The Power of Maturity* Rabbi Louis Binstock wrote that mature people are happy by having senses of:

- Being–Expressing who we are and living accordingly makes us happy.
- Belonging—When we feel we are a part of something bigger and greater, like family, associations, community, and groups, we are happy.
- Growing—We feel happy when we are growing to become our best.
- Meaning—Fulfilling a purpose for living, such as pursuing and cultivating our talent, makes us happy.
- Giving—Giving is a self-enlarging and self-enhancing activity. It makes us happy to give.

There are three sources of happiness:

1. Inward source of happiness—our soul or the love or God inside us. This is the happiness that is constant, and we carry it with us all the time.
2. Outward source of happiness—the love we give out to people brings happiness to our lives. Also, the work that we do to make a difference in others makes us happy.
3. Our philosophy in life—When we are living a good philosophy in life and able to live the way we want to live, and living our best, we are happy.

German philosopher Immanuel Kant (1724–1804) wrote, "It is God's will, not merely that we should be happy, but that we should make ourselves happy."

Here are my personal reminders for making myself happy:

- Live simply.
- Do not carry negative emotions such as fear and worry.
- Always remember that God is in you, and God is in everyone.
- Live in the present and make each day as your best day.

When we are not emotionally mature, our happiness depends primarily on satisfying what gives us pleasure at the present moment—we are hedonistic. Like children, we are happy when people give us what we want, take care of our comfort, and provide us with whatever we need. We focus our energy on becoming rich or famous or powerful—for self-importance.

As we mature, we learn the wisdom passed down to us by Jesus Christ, the Buddha, Lao-tzu, and other sages who teach us that emotional and spiritual maturity (love) are what brings lasting happiness.

The Gospel of Matthew, chapters five to seven is the Sermon on the Mount, which begins with what is called the Beatitudes. Jesus Christ gave us guideposts and inspiration for what to do to be happy in this world. He gave us comfort and encouragement to live a good life. Jesus spoke to them, saying, "I am the light of the world. Whoever follows me will not walk in darkness, but will have the light of life." (John 8:12, *New American Bible*)

In writing the Beatitudes, my poems are actually more like prose than poetry. I was influenced to write in this format after I read *The Life of Saint Francis of Assisi by St. Bonaventure* (1221–1274). The author was an Italian theologian and monk, commissioned by the Franciscan order to write the official biography of St. Francis. He wrote some prose in poetry form. It complemented and elaborated the essay.

The Beatitudes are:

- "Blessed are the poor in spirit, for theirs is the Kingdom of Heaven."

Most people are lucky if they realize that we need God in their lives. We are sinners and weak and need to focus on our spiritual development hand-in-hand with secular pursuits. We are human beings with basic needs to live on this earth, but we should value our spiritual growth and development more than physical things. Worldly happiness is often fleeting and short-lived. St. Augustine wrote, "Our hearts are restless until they rest in You (God)."

> I need you, God
> I am as the skies needing
> the sun.
> I need your love,
> your guidance, your mercy.
> Without you, God,
> I live in the dark.
>
> I am happy because I have You,
> because your Spirit is always with me—
> my life blooms

- "Blessed are they who mourn, for they will be comforted."

We experience personal losses. Tragedies, accidents, illnesses, and deaths happen every day. We need to mourn our losses. Jesus Christ told us that He will comfort us. He makes us realize that losses are one of the givens in this life. Life and love without pain is not of this world.

> Sometimes
> I remember something
> that is so painful.
> The pain is sharp
> like an open wound.
>
> Sometimes it paralyzes me.
>
> My world is black
> until my frontal lobes work;
> until my spirit enlightens me.

I offer my sufferings:
to you, God;
for myself,
for all the people I love.

I am at peace
to live in pain.
It is all right
for me to suffer.

God is comforting me.
God is soothing me
like the warm breeze,
the beautiful sceneries,
like my grandsons playing,
like my grandsons laughing.

God is comforting me.
I am with my son
and I am with you, God.

"God is my shepherd.
I shall not want...." (23rd Psalm) (See Appendix—B)

My Spirit
is connected
with you, Edward.
I carry you
wherever I go
in all seasons,
night and day.

- "Blessed are the meek, for they will inherit the land."

We need to be humble and accept our lot in life. We are not privileged people. We are ordinary human beings with no reason to be arrogant. Everything we have is a gift from God. We have to get rid of our pride and prejudices. We love and respect everybody. We are all humans who live a temporary existence, ordinary and sinners. We do not prejudge people by their outward appearances.

> I live an ordinary life
> I am humble.
> I treat people with respect.
> I do not demand.
> I am unconditionally accepting
> of people and things.
> I share my feelings
> but
> I am not easily angered.
> I forgive others
> And I forgive myself.
> I am grateful for everything—
> I am happy.

- "Blessed are they who hunger and thirst for righteousness, for they will be satisfied."

We have virtues and values that are handed to us from generation to generation. We should voice our opinion and try to do what is right. We should prevent people from doing wrong. For example, I think that abortion is wrong. Spend time convincing the person who plans on having one to change her mind. Equal rights for women in the workforce, and segregation between whites and blacks has been abolished because we have spoken up for righteousness.

> It is good for us
> To do what is right,
> what is just.
> It may be very difficult now
> but we will not have regrets

later on.
Good will triumph over evil.

•   "Blessed are the merciful, for they will be shown mercy."

Christ's overall message is to have mercy.

God is merciful, and we can show mercy as Jesus Christ is merciful to us.

We are happy when we live with compassion in our hearts and help those who are less fortunate.

Buddha's teaching is also about mercy. Because we are ignorant of the truth, we should have compassion for one another.

> I remember
> Someone said,
> "Don't kick the person
> who has fallen down;
> help lift him/her up."

•   "Blessed are the clean of heart, for they will see God."

When our eyes are focused on God instead of worldly things, we have fewer problems.

When we try our best to live with humility, simplicity and forgiveness; our energy is not used up by destructive thoughts and feelings. We are more prone to see truth, goodness, and beauty. We see God. We see Love.

> Life
> We should live
> with empathy
> and forgiveness.
>
> We can ask God for forgiveness.
> We can walk with comfort and joy.

- "Blessed are the peacemakers, for they will be called children of God."

We should live with peace in ourselves, and our relationships. We should help people to live in peace whenever we can.

> Peace
> It is amazing how non-violence
> changes the world
> for the better.
> Gandhi was inspired
> by reading the Beatitudes,
> and by reading Tolstoy.

- "Blessed are they who are persecuted for the sake of righteousness, for theirs is the Kingdom of Heaven."

The twelve apostles, except for St. John and St. Jude Thaddaeus, died as martyrs. Their faith was so great that they did not relinquish it even when faced with martyrdom.

> Faith
> Be true to yourself always
> But respect others' beliefs
> That differ from your own.

The Beatitudes are Christian spiritual guides to a happy life. Once we live with the Beatitudes, we can live with inner joy. A joyful life is full of pain. Pain and joy go hand in hand in this life. Because I had exquisite joy living with my son in this world, I had indescribable pain when he died until God healed me. God made me realize that my son's spirit is with me. He is no longer here physically, but our thoughts and spirits are together. I can think of him, I can talk to him, and he inspires me to be my best and do good things for his sake.

Like a beautiful painting, with its many colors, shades and shadows, a beautiful life includes pain, heartaches, and struggles. Being happy means living with those contrasts. My ninety-year-old friend told me that she has no complaints about her life; she accepts the good and the bad things and is grateful every day. She also said, "I am making my life my best composition."

How we treat ourselves and others contributes much to our happiness. When we have unconditional self-love and unconditional love of others, we live with happiness. Love and closeness of family, friends, coworkers, neighbors, and the world bring permanent happiness and inner joy to our lives. Relationships enhance the quality of our life; they are also our support system in times of stress. They amplify our joy and dilute our grief. When we make someone happy, we will be happy, too. Whatever good we do to anyone will bring good to our life. We are the world. We are interrelated. We can do small things for the world each day. Mother Teresa of Calcutta wrote, "We can do small things with great love." Buddha wrote, "Live with compassion and forgiveness." The Dalai Lama wrote, "If you want others to be happy, practice compassion. If you want to be happy, practice compassion." To live a happy life—give. We do not expect our relationships to give to us; we are responsible for our own life choices, needs, and happiness.

Some thoughts and behaviors we can cultivate that add to our happiness are as follows:

- Always remember the good things and blessings in your life, and share them; reflect on happy memories.
- Always remember that everything in this world passes, but you have an eternal soul.
- Take care of your health and avoid unnecessary stress.
- Always have a positive mental attitude; find the advantages for every disadvantage.

- You are never alone; God is with you.
- Reflect on love as written by St. Paul (1 Corinthians 13:1–13) (See Appendix B.)
- Enjoy things like beauty, nature, music, pets, scents, spices, hobbies, reading, good TV programs, magazines, books, writing letters, and physical activities.
- Take the time to be with and enjoy your family and friends.
- Know the purpose of your life and align your goals with that; practice self-discipline and live your dreams.
- Believe in yourself. Be true to yourself. Live your truth and core values.
- Live with courage, creativity, hope, and effort. Use and develop your God-given gifts.
- Accept the suffering and pain in life. Go ahead: smile, sing, laugh, play, and feel better.
- Live in the present moment.
- Get or create the job you love. Enjoy your work.
- Follow the Ten Commandments.
- Use mature ego defenses and develop emotional maturity to cope with the difficult and painful occurrences in your life.

Angelus Silesius wrote, "Where are you running to? Stay where you are, heaven is within you. If you look elsewhere you will never find it." Like love, happiness is within us. We are capable of being happy anywhere and everywhere we are.

Happiness can also be transmitted through our genes. There is a hereditary gene that makes people become inherently happy and also a gene that is linked to depression (Lancet, 2013). A gene found in women, but not in men, appears to be linked to an upbeat personality. The low expression of the gene monoamine oxidase A (MAOA) is associated with self-reported happiness in women (http://psychcentral.com/news, August 29, 2012). Scientists discovered that MAOAI (monoamine oxidase A inhibitor) in women regulates an enzyme that breaks down brain neurotransmitters such as serotonin and dopamine, the "feel good" chemical targeted by many antidepressants (http://mayoclinic.com 2013). The gene allows larger amounts of these neurotransmitters to stay in the brain and boost mood.

Living with Edward in 1996
The skies open wide.
The sun shines its perfect rays.
The blue jay sings each day
and each night.
I feel my endorphins flowing;
each day my spirit beams
with joy.

Our activities
are routine
as the moon and sun,
our movements
predictable
and soothing
as the tides returning
to the shores.

We are each other's teachers
of life.
Edward also teaches me the English language.
He says, "Let me show you, Mom."
We share the same passion
for learning, for appreciating beauty,
for laughing, for crying.

Each time we live together,
once again
the wild white water lilies
bloom.

I continue journeying through the bumpy roads of my life. I continue to develop myself to be strong and able to cope with and overcome obstacles. How I respond to events is what makes a difference in my life. The quality of my journey depends on me.

You can live a happy and fulfilled life despite continuous challenges, regardless of how hard they may be. You can learn how to handle and have the right amount of stress so that you are able to live as a healthy being.

SELF-ACTUALIZATION

As human beings we need to survive, grow, and self-realize. When we reach self-actualization, we experience life like a child, being who we truly are. We are mature but childlike. We live our true selves; we listen to our feelings; we are free, creative, and in pursuit of our talents.

Abraham Maslow wrote in *Toward the Psychology of Being* that we need to fulfill our basic needs before we can self-realize and achieve our potential as persons. This is the usual pattern of development, though, there have been people like Rembrandt and Van Gogh who lived in extreme poverty, unable to fulfill their basic needs, but were still able to fulfill their highest creative potentials. I have also witnessed people in the barrio in the Philippines who were living in extreme poverty but who became great painters.

There are people who spend their whole lives working continuously just to fulfill their basic needs. They never grow to love and give of themselves. They remain selfish and self-centered. These people need help to grow and develop. Selfish people are difficult to love, yet only through loving them will they grow, change, and develop their ability to love.

Maslow identified fifteen characteristics of self-actualized people. They

- perceive reality efficiently and can tolerate uncertainty;
- accept themselves and others for what they are;

- are spontaneous in thought and action;
- are problem centered rather than not self-centered;
- have an unusual sense of humor;
- are able to look at life objectively;
- are highly creative;
- are resistant to enculturation, but not purposely unconventional;
- are concerned for the welfare of humanity;
- are capable of deep appreciation of basic life experience;
- establish deep, satisfying interpersonal relationships with a few people;
- have peak experiences;
- have a need for privacy;
- have democratic attitudes; and
- have strong moral and ethical standards.

Peak experiences are experiences of intense happiness and joy. When I reread some of my poems, I experience extremely happy feelings. Watching my grandsons having fun as they play brings me this experience, too. There are many little things that give me this experience, such as seeing the flowers bloom suddenly, hearing the birds singing, seeing the heron standing straight on the edge of the pond, or watching my dog lying down peacefully next to me.

I have a close friend who is always laughing. She always comes up with funny comments. She is one of my self-actualized friends. She said, "I live to bring joy to people." Once I called her up and told her that I am selling raffle tickets for my niece's school and asked her if she would like to purchase one. She said, "I will take three, my hands are itchy." It is an old belief that having an itchy palm is a sign that you will come into money.

Saints have varied lives, but they all lived their best selves. Some were formally educated, others were not. Some grew up in affluence, others grew up in poverty. Some died young, others lived to their old age. Saints are good examples of self-actualized human beings. You do not have to be rich, famous, a genius, or powerful to be self-actualized. But you have to be the best person that you can be.

Self-actualization

Live as you are,
Whether you are like a tree, a shrub, or a water lily—live.
Be who you are, develop your best self.
Grow whatever you can be, keep becoming your best self.

Stay happy and create;
Appreciate what you have made
Of yourself.
Keep brightening your world, each day.
Keep brightening the world like the sun
That keeps nourishing the world—
Like love.

Stay happy.
No matter what comes your way.
Live your best.

CHAPTER 4

―――――― ❈ ――――――

Emotions

Growing emotionally and living with
emotional maturity or mature ego
defenses is a lifetime endeavor.

I N THIS CHAPTER, I will discuss our emotions and the
things that influence them: emotional maturity, emotional
growth, emotional intelligence-raising emotionally mature
and emotionally intelligent children, processing our negative
emotions-and a description of the levels of our consciousness.
When we are emotionally mature or intelligent and have higher
levels of consciousness we function with optimum energy.

EMOTIONAL GROWTH, MATURITY, OR INTELLIGENCE

Emotions can propel us into action. They can be the stimuli
that make us do good things as well as bad or destructive things.
Emotional maturity or growing emotionally means being aware of
our feelings whether we are happy, sad, angry, or anxious, and that
we are aware of what we seek. We are able to express our feelings
appropriately. We can delight in our joyful feelings; acknowledge
our uncomfortable feelings, such as sadness and anger; and channel
them into constructive or creative activities (sublimation).

Christine was so devastated when her dog died. She felt better
making a scrapbook of her dog's pictures and plans to write a
children's book afterward.

I use self-discipline (suppression) to stop myself from saying something that I will regret later. When I am angry with someone or I do not like what that person is doing, I try to understand that other people have different ways of looking at things. Another's reality is different from the way I look at things. When I can anticipate (anticipation) someone's idiosyncrasies, I am not bothered by them.

Juan is from Columbia, and he is almost always late for his office appointments. He is never punctual because since childhood he has never been used to following a set appointment time. Because I was aware of his way of keeping his appointments, I anticipated his behavior and reminded him ahead of time to be punctual.

Another example: If we are very busy at work, we can continue our work until we are done. We comfort ourselves by anticipating a future vacation.

When we love (altruism) better, we can love a person unconditionally and can make a distinction between their outward appearances and behaviors and their unique selves. Love is the hallmark of emotional maturity. It is a cure for pride and prejudice, destructive impulses, or other less constructive and less adaptive coping skills. Also, if we lose someone we deeply love, we can channel our sad feelings by doing some volunteer work and helping those who are less fortunate (altruism).

When we experience an embarrassing situation, we can share the incident with a friend and laugh about it (humor). One time, I was wearing a loose half-slip and my slip just came down to my ankles while I was walking to get a drink at a party. I just hurriedly took it off and put my slip into my pocketbook. As soon as I got a chance, I called my girlfriend and we laughed! She said, "I know you do not like to wear tight clothing. At least it was not your panties that fell off."

These five mature ego defenses are simple skills, but they take time, effort, and practice to implement. If you did not learn these mature ego defenses in your growing up years and were unable to use them unconsciously or automatically, or if you are currently undergoing a lot of stress and become less mature, you can use mature ego defenses consciously by choice and apply them daily in your life. You can exert effort to process and channel your uncomfortable emotions into constructive activities, so that you become effective in your work, relationships, and in solving your problems.

Aristotle wrote in *The Nicomachean Ethics,* "Anyone can become angry—that is easy. But to be angry with the right person, to the right degree, at the right time, for the right purpose, and in the right way—this is not easy."

In Daniel Goleman's book *Emotional Intelligence*, he cited a study of four-year-old children who were given marshmallows and were told that if they postponed eating their marshmallows, they could have double the number of marshmallows later on. They were followed up ten years later. Those children who were able to postpone eating their marshmallows turned out to be more successful than those who were unable to postpone eating the marshmallows. The ability to suppress (self-discipline) one's impulses early on in life seem to be a good predictor of success later in life.

Emotional maturity means being a good person. We reflect on our thoughts and behaviors periodically, repent for our wrongdoing, and correct ourselves to better ourselves.

Every day, Jose spends time reflecting on his life and examining his own conscience. When you see him, his eyes have a glow. He also told me that he recites the Holy Rosary every day and reflects on its mystery. He attests that reflecting on the mysteries and life of Jesus Christ always brings him peace. He vouches that Jesus Christ is truly the Prince of Peace.

Friendship is important in developing emotional maturity. We should cultivate intimate relationships that edify us and associate with those who inspire us and make us better. Once we have constructive loving relationships, we need to take time to nurture them.

Each person is unique. Respect your friends for their uniqueness. You can walk hand in hand in the same direction, nurturing each other's intellectual or spiritual growth, growing together. It takes time and effort to cultivate friendship. We need to learn to be loyal and trustworthy ourselves in order to acquire friends who are also loyal and trustworthy.

Emotional maturity means continuous growth. Emotional growth means having empathy. Put yourself in the other person's shoes and feel how the other person feels. Empathy can lead to altruism and compassion. When we get along well with people, we develop social deftness. When we have empathy, we become good at sizing up people and social situations. This is how we develop and choose friends who become our loyal, intimate, and trusted true friends.

Emotional growth involves optimism. Look at setbacks as temporary things that can be reversed by time and effort. People who lack emotional growth can be pessimists and consider failures as permanent. Discouraged people lack the desire to do things to improve their situation. The seventeen skill sets to learn and develop for living well are roadmaps for optimism. Make a habit of contemplating about and applying these qualities and you will be more optimistic.

Norman Vincent Peale wrote forty-six books based on the Bible and coauthored two books together with the psychiatrist Dr. Smiley Blanton. Peale's most famous book is *The Power of Positive Thinking*. Positive thinking is seeing the good side of things and finding the advantages for every disadvantage. It is accepting our humanness and imperfections, the good and bad things in life, and focusing on the good. Positive thinking means having a strong faith in God. When we trust and surrender our life to God, we develop confidence that things will be alright. Positive thinking is believing in ourselves.

Steve Jobs is one example of someone who had a strong self-belief. He strongly believed in his creative mind; he was able to put together things that changed our way of life.

In the New Testament, Jesus said, "Do not be afraid, for I am with you." In the Old Testament, God said, "Do not fear, for I am with you; do not be dismayed, for I am your God. I will strengthen you and help you; I will uphold you with my righteous right hand." (Isaiah 41:10, New International Version)

Emotional growth also involves self-motivation. Rely on yourself to do what is good for you. Do not depend on others to motivate you to do things. Don't be lazy. Some people spend many hours watching TV just to pass the time and complain that they are bored. I pray for those people. I pray to God to give them the courage or power to find something worthwhile to live for and do each day. If you have a problem, work on finding a solution yourself. You should not wait for luck or for other people to solve your problems. Persevere by yourself and do the work you need to do.

Emotional growth also involves having a passion for life and the desire to live to the fullest in the present moment. Do not dwell on the past or the future. Be aware of the ups and downs in life. You may have sadness and disappointments as well as good fortune in life. Accept that your human condition can be very difficult. Our life experiences help us become better and more understanding people. We grow wiser by overcoming the difficult things we encounter in life.

Emotional growth includes humility. We can disclose our experiences when they will help others to see things better. Share your life, your humanness. We have to learn to be humble. The more aware we are of our own faults and weaknesses, the more tolerant and accepting we are of other people's faults.

My girlfriend has a daughter who is well-educated, famous, and humble. She describes her daughter's endearing qualities saying, "She is always accepting and understanding of people's mistakes. She is never critical, arrogant, or self-centered."

Emotional growth involves perseverance. No matter how long it rains and thunders, eventually the sun will shine. When we decide to do something regardless of the difficulty, we keep working until we accomplish our goals. We find many venues for doing the task and we do not give up easily. Writing this book was not easy for me, but I kept on writing. I have been writing this book for over four years now.

We learn to grow emotionally and become mature by ourselves, as well as through our environment. When we are raised by parents who acknowledge our feelings and support the expression of our feelings, we become more aware of our emotions.

One of my cousins, an only child, called to invite me to the anniversary remembrance of his mother's death. He mentioned that he was able to mourn, express, and accept his loss because he is close to all of us—his immediate and extended family and friends. Also, his mother had told him when she was still alive, "No matter what happens, you can cope with anything if you live with trust and have faith in the Lord."

Emotional maturity, growth and intelligence are part of our reasoning and emotional capabilities. It requires effective communication between the emotional right and rational left centers of our brain. This develops and improves with use. J. M. Stewart wrote that emotional intelligence has existed since humankind existed. In the nineteenth century, we called it *horse sense* and in the twentieth century, we call it *street smarts*. Charles Darwin wrote that the smartest creatures are the ones that are most adaptable. We adapt well when we are emotionally mature, emotionally growing, and emotionally intelligent.

Robert has been very popular in his company. He became the president of his company in twelve years. He never misses a day of work; he has been married for twenty years, and has three successful and popular children. Great leaders have good emotional intelligence. Emotional intelligence accounts for 90 percent of what separates good leaders from average ones.

Daniel Goleman, PhD, wrote that schools all over the world are implementing emotional intelligence (EI) in their curriculum. *Intelligence quotient* (IQ) is a genetic gift and changes very little over time, but emotional intelligence can be learned and developed and influences the success of one's relationships, career, physical, and mental health. It is proving to be a more accurate predictor of our potential for happiness and success in life.

Reuben Bar-On, PhD, a clinical psychologist, developed the EQ-i (Emotional Quotient Inventory) after eighteen years of research. It is the first accepted measurement of emotional intelligence and people have been subjected to the test in thirty countries. There is also another accepted test called the Mayer-Salovey-Caruso Emotional Intelligence Test (MSCEIT 2.0). Four criteria are used to measure the MSCEIT. They are: the (1) ability to identify the other person or the environment's emotions (empathy), (2) the ability to use emotions, (3) understanding emotions, and (4) managing emotions.

Raising children to become emotionally mature and emotionally intelligent

As a mother I have learned that children who are raised to be in touch with their feelings and have the ability to express them have a good chance to grow up as successful adults. This is because they are understood, validated in their experiences, and feel valued. At an early age, they are nurtured and learn qualities needed to become emotionally mature as presented in this book. They experience negative emotions and pain in life, but they are able to adapt. They learn and start to use mature ego defenses during their developmental years. Many are popular in school. Their classmates are often fond of them. They learn cooperation and teamwork. Most children experience both defeat and victory early on and grow from these experiences. Unfortunately, according to the famous family therapist, Virginia Satir, only about 5 percent of families are functional. Most of us grew up in varying degrees of dysfunction. But we can learn on our own to acquire emotional maturity. Hillary Rodham Clinton appropriately titled her book about raising children, *It Takes a Village.*

The abilities to identify, use, understand, and manage emotions and to develop compassion and empathy are manifestations of emotional maturity, emotional growth, or emotional intelligence.

MANAGING NEGATIVE EMOTIONS

Destructive thoughts, feelings, and behaviors are part of our human nature. In the Judeo-Christian tradition, God created Adam and Eve in the image and likeness of God (Genesis 1:26–27). God told them, "You may eat indeed of all the trees in the garden, nevertheless of the tree of the knowledge of good and evil you are not to eat, for on the day you eat of it you shall most surely die." (Genesis 2:16–17, *Jerusalem Bible*) Eve was tempted by the serpent to eat the rich fruit of the forbidden tree, and she in turn convinced Adam to eat the fruit. Because Adam and Eve disobeyed God, they were expelled from paradise and their lives ended in death. In this allegory, since we came from Adam and Eve, death is our destiny; destructive thoughts, feelings, behaviors, suffering, and pain are also part of our nature and destiny. We lose our image and likeness of God. We are sinful and mortal beings.

God gave us free will; we can choose either good or bad. We can choose to do good and be good or we can choose to do bad things. Bad thinking usually precedes bad behavior. David Burn, MD's book *Feeling Good: The New Mood Therapy* teaches people how to restructure their negative thinking. We can acknowledge negative thoughts and feelings and redirect them to constructive venues. Mastering and changing oneself is not easy; it takes time and continuous work throughout a lifetime; but we can work at it as long as we can still think. Mastering ourselves means developing emotional maturity. Self-mastery includes handling stress since stress affects our ability to use mature or constructive ego defenses.

Negative thoughts usually lead to destructive behavior.

For example, Edwin is forty years old and dropped out of school at fifteen. He is a pessimist and has been jobless. He smokes two packs of cigarettes every day, drinks beer, and steals money from his parents' house. He has no motivation at all to find a job. His two brothers and two sisters, who gave up on him, do not even talk to him.

Jessie blamed his parents for not giving him the opportunity to go to college. He lived a miserable life on welfare, and later he developed alcoholism. He was this way for ten years. Fortunately, another person, who was in recovery from using alcohol, invited him to attend the Alcoholics Anonymous (AA) program. It turned his life around. He spent three years attending the program faithfully. He came to my office for a physical for work, and he told me that he owed his transformed life to the AA program. He currently works as a home health aide, helping a mentally challenged child. He continues to attend the AA meetings close to his home, and feels the community also gives him a sense of belonging.

Emotions (Edward edited this)
Emotions reside
in our conscious
and unconscious mind
as seashells dwell
on shores and within the ocean.

But we are often
not aware
of all our emotions;
we know only
what is in our conscious mind,
we see only
what is on the surface
of the ocean—

the outer layer
of the skies,
the outside glitter
of the sands.

We are often
not aware
of the emotions
that live
in our unconscious mind
as we do not see
the vast number of stars
until we wait for night to unfold.

We must therefore spend
a lot of time
to be,
to feel,
to keep on experiencing our feelings;
to allow the unconscious
to become conscious,
to let winter
become summer.

Only then
will we discover the pain and joy
that allow us to create
and live;
the emotions that make us truly happy—
Love

Here is some fuel for meditation:

• Meditate on the description of love. Refer to the table on
   page 57.
• Meditate on loving yourself.
• Meditate on loving others for the love of God. (Remember
   that God is in all of us.)

Meditate on the description on love as a checklist for loving yourself. When you have a problem with someone, instead of being angry or criticizing that one's behavior, think of ways to love the person. Use the items on the left-hand side as ways of thinking about and responding to the other person. Do these things as a way of loving God.

Here are common negative emotions:

- *Fear* covers love. Most uncomfortable feelings, such as anger and anxiety, come from fear. You can be loving and fearful at the same time, but your ability to love can be diminished by your fear. Norman Vincent Peale, in his book *Bible Power of Successful Living,* wrote, "Reading the Bible is the sure cure for fear and stress." Herbert W. Armstrong wrote, "If we are to enjoy the good things in life—freedom from fears and worries ... the very source of their supply is the Great God." Living with faith in God, imitating the life of Jesus Christ—becoming a loving person—prevents us from doing things that often make us fearful. Trusting God and having the faith to accept God's will also give us strength and peace. I always remember my mother, who always lived without fear because of her strong faith in God. My maternal aunt is still alive at one hundred years old, and her life is centered on God and prayers. She lives a simple, peaceful, fearless, and productive life even at her age. Whenever we visit her, she always makes sure that our favorite fruits are on the table. It is her way of showing love for us.
- *Envy* is a destructive thought and feeling. It means wanting what another person has. Instead of being self-reliant and using our energy to improve ourselves, we waste it focusing on another's life. Get rid of envy and use your mind to make the best of your life. When you are childish,

you envy. Grow up and work on becoming physically and emotionally self-reliant. If you contemplate the message of the ninth and tenth of the Ten Commandments, you will learn not to think of what other people have, and will become a better person by not envying and putting your energy into constructive things.

- *Anger* is often a destructive emotion. People can destroy themselves or others because of their anger. Love is the antidote for anger. Whenever I am angry with what another person is doing, I always remember to forgive. I say to myself, "If God can forgive, I should be forgiving, too." Appreciate the good things about others, and overlook their faults. Be good and do good things for the people who do not treat you well. This is sometimes hard to do, but with practice you can do it.

However, anger can also be a useful guide to doing constructive things. Anger can give us insight into the need to change ourselves. Until I was around thirty years old, I would become angry easily. I realized that I should become more self-reliant or less dependent. Accepting responsibility for my angry feelings made me grow and develop more self-esteem as well.

- *Narcissism*: Thinking of one's own needs without considering others and not having the ability to feel what another person feels is the hallmark of narcissism.

Edwin busied himself doing what he enjoyed doing and spent the family income by buying whatever he wanted. Since he handled the household finances, he spent all of it for what he wanted. He had no sense of the Golden Rule. He lacked empathy. Pride, greed, lust, and deceit are common characteristics of narcissism. He was unaware that what he was doing was wrong and unfair to his family. He believed that his income was his and that his wife's income was also his. To him there was nothing wrong with what he was doing.

My brother in the Philippines told me this story: A grandfather told his grandson, "We have two wolves in our hearts and minds fighting for attention all the time." His grandson asked, "Grandpa, why are they fighting? Who gets more attention and wins?" The grandfather answered, "The two wolves are good and bad. Whichever wolf we feed more wins. If we think and do more good things in life, then good will prevail and we will have a good life. If we dwell on and do bad things in life, then we will have a bad life."

The seventeen skill sets are useful in handling negative emotions. Any of these attributes can be good food for your mind. Select any of the qualities that apply to your present situation. For example, if you are angry, process your anger by understanding the situation, being patient, or using your sense of humor. Horace Walpole wrote, "Life is a comedy for those who think." At another time, you might think of faith as an appropriate choice. You might find reading the Bible or any religious writing to be inspiring. When I am busy, the quickest ego defense that I use is humor. I make a habit of seeing the funny side of things. I also memorized some funny stories, and I recall them whenever I find my situation to be upsetting. I use humor as an ego defense to make myself feel better.

About the tabulation:

Write any disturbing thoughts or feelings or behaviors you have on top of the chart and meditate on the solutions in the left hand column that are applicable to you at the moment.

Examples of some negative thoughts and feelings are pride, envy, greed, lust, deceit, anger, laziness, prejudice, and fear.

Seventeen skill sets	Pride	Envy	Greed	Lust	deceit	Anger	Laziness	Prejudice	Fear
Altruism (love)									
Suppression (self-discipline)									
Anticipation									
Sublimation (creativity)									
Humor									
Faith in God									
Acceptance of Suffering									
Peace and joy									
Self – Love and Self – Esteem									
Courage									
Hope									
Work									
Understanding									
Play									
Happiness									
Energy									
Handling Stress									

To summarize, you can handle your negative thoughts and feelings and make them constructive by:

- Being responsible for yourself, being emotionally mature, and using the seventeen skill sets in this book.
- Handling your stress each day.
- Acknowledging thoughts and feelings, being self-aware through contemplation or self-reflection, exercising self-control when it is destructive to express thoughts or feelings, responding creatively, or being proactive. If someone is angry with you, do not automatically react in anger. Take the time to evaluate the situation and choose a response that is constructive to everybody involved, responding with the seventeen skill sets enumerated on the left side of the chart. Again, not all characteristics apply to one particular problem. Choose and use the ones that apply.
- Doing positive things such as reading and meditating on prayers, Judeo-Christian Bible scriptures, and quotes found in Appendixes B and C.
- Repeating affirmations and visualizations, and feeling the emotions you are feeling.
- Living a loving and prayerful life.

Flowers
Why is it so sudden
When it blooms?
Why all these colors?
Pink, yellow, purple, red, even green.
Why all these fragrances?
Sweet, soothing, relaxing, unforgettable.
The answers are within the flowers
As the answers to our feelings are within us.

Healing our negative emotions
We need to love ourselves unconditionally.
We need to give and forgive,

Value who and what we are, as we are.
Our self-esteem is unconditional,
And we love ourselves wholeheartedly.
Our self-love and self-esteem are not dependent on others,
Nor on outward appearances and success.

We live a life that makes us like ourselves.
We depend on ourselves for our happiness.
For living what we want
Like a gardenia living through the nourishment from
the sun,
Exuding its own beauty and fragrance.

We are responsible for what we think,
How we feel and what we do.
We let others
Be responsible
For themselves,
For what they think and what they do.

We are individual pebbles,
But we are also together—
We are the seas, the winds.
We are the world.

Breakthrough (Edward edited this, too)
A long journey
unnoticed by others,
each step felt
painfully from our epidermis
to the nucleolus
of every cell.

Problem-solving
requires
our whole being's strength, other people's love,
God's grace.

We do not become winners
without our relentless
and strongest effort.
A mountain cannot be moved
effortlessly;
we cannot break
a stone while sleeping.

It isn't uncommon
to stop
in the middle
and die unnoticed
like a tree rotting
from the inside.

We mine the rocks
Until we find diamonds;
We work till our limbic system
Knows we made a breakthrough.

Two Children
I was with two children
At the hospital lobby waiting
For the result
Of their mother's operation.

Their eyes were wide opened.
Their mouths were tightly closed.
They were both standing still
With their hands held together.

There were no answers
To my questions
No matter what I asked,
No matter how hard
I tried.

These two children
Had very little

Experience
About life;
They did not understand
But felt
And expressed
Emotions
That were real.

They remind me
That we can always express
Ourselves—
Validate our feelings
Honest like
Children.

To My 92-Year-Old Patient

I want you to tell me
Your passion,
Your dreams,
Your fears
Before dawn comes.

I want you to tell me
The heartbreaks
That turn
Rain into sheaths of ice.

I want you to sing
The song you once sang
That massaged your soul.

I want you to write
The love stories
That make
Your life grand.

Most of all,
I want you to continue
Writing poetry.

I want you to keep
Writing words
That melt your emotions
Into gold.

LEVELS OF CONSCIOUSNESS

Around the middle of the twentieth century, Dr. George Goodheart pioneered the field of *applied kinesiology*. Kinesiology is the study of muscles and their movements. He learned that organic foods increase the strength of certain indicator muscles—they use the deltoid muscles in the arms in their studies, whereas artificial foods such as artificial sweeteners weaken these muscles. In the 1970s, Dr. John Diamond further discovered that indicator muscles would strengthen or weaken not only on physical stimuli, but on positive or negative emotional and intellectual stimuli as well. Dr. Diamond wrote a book, *Your Body Doesn't Lie,* describing how muscle testing is done.

Dr. David Hawkins implemented Dr. Diamond's method in his research on levels of consciousness through muscle testing. He was able to discern truth versus falsehood through muscle testing and measure subjects' levels of consciousness. He wrote a book entitled *Power Versus Force* in which he explained that the higher a person's level of consciousness, the more power that person has in life. He mapped Jesus Christ, Buddha, and Krishna as having the highest level of consciousness, which was measured at around 1,000 on the scale he constructed. The teachings of Jesus Christ, Buddha, and Krishna, as calculated by Dr. Hawkins, showed pure consciousness and enlightenment. His calculations started at 20, where people feel shame, misery and humiliation. The levels moved up to 30, where feelings of guilt is experienced; level 50 is apathy; level 75 is grief; level 100 is desire; level 150 is anger; level 175 is pride; and level 200 is courage. At the level of 200 truth exists and empowerment starts.

Unconditional love is above 500. The emotions of affirmation, trust, optimism, forgiveness, understanding, reverence, serenity, and bliss are experienced upon moving up to even higher levels. Enlightenment and ineffable positive emotions are the highest levels that human beings can achieve.

Dr. Hawkins wrote, "The collective level of consciousness of mankind remained at 190 (below the level of power and truth) for many centuries and curiously, only jumped to its current level of 207 within the last decade" (1995).

I often meditate on the levels of consciousness and focus my thoughts and emotions at levels 200 and above. I find this to be very effective in achieving peace and joy, having more energy, and engaging in constructive activities each day.

ENERGY

We use our energy to live. Our sense of well-being and how much we are truly living depends on how much energy we have and how we use it. When we are focused on doing what we decide to do in the present moment, without thinking of other things, we are living fully. However, if we are preoccupied with worries and emotions such as anger, hatred, pride, prejudice, envy, greed, sloth, and lust, which are lower levels of our consciousness, we waste our energy and feel we have no energy. We are tired all the time. If we are not using our energy constructively, we are not fully living.

We have more energy when:

- We love our life and people. Love is the energy of life. When we love, we live. Look at the pictures of Mother Teresa of Calcutta. Doesn't she exude peace and love? Read about the enormous work she has done. People who love life and are loving usually are full of energy.

- We ask God to give us energy, to give us life. "We receive what we ask." Faith in God gives us energy.
- Our thoughts, emotions and souls are aligned in one positive direction.
- We live a virtuous life. There are virtues we can make habitual that will make our life more functional. Some of these are humility, truthfulness, cleanliness, orderliness, self-discipline, industry, positive mental attitude, resolve, frugality, moderation, right judgment, and charity. Benjamin Franklin, in his autobiography, wrote that he tabulated the virtues he wanted to acquire and checked them daily until they became part of his character. The more virtues we live with, the fewer preventable problems we have to deal with in life.

I am not as disciplined as I want to be. I have an index card in my wallet where I write a daily to-do list and read the virtues that I want to develop to improve my day-to-day life. Most people are good at some virtues and need improvement in others. We can all work on our individual deficiencies.

When we acquire many virtues, we are more relaxed, less stressed out, and more productive. Notice people who are accomplishing good things for themselves and others. They are able to do their task because they are usually focused and use their thoughts, emotions, and spiritual energies constructively. They live with goodness in their hearts and souls. Jeremy Lin's advice to the 2012 Stuyvesant High School graduates was to "enjoy yourself, love what you are doing." Enjoyment comes from love. When we enjoy what we do, we have more energy.

- We are inspired, motivated or have a worthy goal. Ask yourself, "What is the reason for living life? What do I live for?" Most people want to be happy; what are the things that make you happy? A proverb says, "What you would die for are the reasons you live for."

- We are physically active, eat healthy, and work on maintaining health to have more energy to do things.

This life energy is called *prana* in Hindu, *chi* in Chinese, and *ki* in Japanese. It is good to be aware of our present energy. When we have a lot of healthy energy, we live more and do more; we accomplish more with our life. I believe that our constructive energy comes from God. Norman Vincent Peale wrote, "God is the source of all energy in the universe—atomic energy, electrical energy, and spiritual energy."

When we are peaceful and in tune with the infinite, energy flows freely to us. When we are emotionally strained by hatred, anger, fear, worry, boredom, resentment, discouragement, and depression, we drain our energy.

A patient told me, "I am constantly doing something or going out somewhere. I have nervous energy, and I am tired all the time." Her nervous energy stops her from doing something constructive for herself and others. She eventually said, "I do not have a goal." She is doing something that prevents her from being true to herself, from healing her emotions, or from doing what she is meant to be doing. Constructive energy is feeling alive, peaceful and happy. It is doing something bigger than ourselves.

PART TWO
STRESS

*Learning about stress is
learning about health*

CHAPTER 5

※

Handling My Personal Stress

> It is effective adaptation to stress
> that permits us to live.
> —George E. Vaillant, M.D.

I LEARNED THE INFORMATION about stress discussed in this chapter from studying medicine, and I use this knowledge in my practice as an internist—a primary care physician. However, I am not writing to diagnose and treat any medical condition. I am writing to show you how to manage stress and how to have the discipline to implement the techniques for doing so—to live well whatever life brings. Consult your own physician for any medical problems you may have.

This chapter illustrates how I handle my personal stress.

Losing my beloved son was the most stressful event that ever happened in my life. I felt paralyzed and did not know what to do from the time he was sick, hospitalized, died, and shortly after that. My world became pitch black after he died. My insights and knowledge about loss coming from my years of helping people overcome their stresses became handy. Nonetheless, my medical knowledge about illnesses and how to manage stress also helped me personally. I also drew a lot of strength from my spirituality. I prayed a lot. My family and friends gave a lot of emotional support, too. My friend called me practically every day to talk about intimate things. I made sure I did more physical activities each day and also made meditation a daily activity in my life. I remembered Edward's poem on meditation, how we discussed various ways of meditating, and how we used to do them together.

Here is a meditation poem that Edward wrote for me on one Mother's Day:

Healing the World from Battery Park

Om Tara
Tu Tara
Ture Svaha
—TIBETAN MANTRA
Draw a deep breath. Hold it. Let it go.
That is the smell of the ocean.
Our forebears hailed from out there. There's a stele
to mark the spot where Minuit exchanged
a mess of beads and trinkets for this island.
He may have thought it proof he was
a clever trader, although if the sky
were sky blue as today, the sunlight's flash
through the bright glass would have been magnificent,
and that might have had tremendous value
in another culture. In another language,
"minuit" is a division of the day.
I've divided my days among a host
of places near the sea. I get a lot
of comfort when I walk on the beach, or through
the narrow streets among a crush of traders.
Sand in my shoes, sand of the Castle
Clinton courtyard where all of New York
turned out of yore to see the Jacksons,
Andrew and his wife. He'd whipped the bloody,
British in the town of New Orleans
and massacred the Creeks. His steely eyes,
as blue as western skies, saw the space I see.
He breathed the same air. There's a little part
of him in me, that wants to drive away
the savages who populate the dark
expanse beyond the porch light's reach.
It takes a trail of Tears to teach

the neighborhood improvement's not the point.
May the breath I draw become a balm
to soothe the exiled people of all times
and lands: the Cherokee, the Jew,
the people of Tibet whose loss brought us
abundant wisdom, the Kulak and the Sioux,
the mother I abandoned and the friends
(a sentence missing) I left behind (my insert)
I'm leaning where it hides. It's in the nectarine
you ate for breakfast, or the thing
you're doing now, not in what you think
you should do or in what comes next.
And it's not in what you think "God" means;
the only certainty is that you're wrong.
Draw a deep breath. Thank you, mother:
Hold the light inside and let it find
the ragged spots, a gentle tongue to probe
for carries. Then expire.
A little part of you is in the wind now,
of brine that clasps you like a lover.
Bless me, father. This is my first
confession: I'm living in the light
at the bottom of the sea of air,
everything I need in a place I share
with everyone. It's in your hands.

I made sure I ate balanced meals every day: three parts complex carbohydrate, one part protein, and one part unsaturated fats (3-1-1) in each meal, and had meals four to five times a day on a regular schedule regardless of whether I felt like eating or not. I ate mainly fresh and organic produce to have maximum nutrients in my diet. I ate one or two servings of fruits and vegetables in each meal.

I had always slept eight hours every night and I kept the same schedule. There are three types of exercises—for flexibility, for strength, and for cardiovascular endurance. I focused on doing aerobic exercises, walking at least twenty minutes every day or every other day. If I didn't do it in the morning, it was more difficult for me to get to it later during the day. I require more discipline to exercise later during the day. Sometimes I had other important things to worry about, such as taking care of my patients, and would end up not having the time to exercise. So I wrote down physical exercise as one of my daily priorities in my to-do list, and did it before taking my shower in the morning. The things I could delegate I asked my secretary to do so that I would have more time for myself. I am very thankful that I had people around me who had been and still are supportive and made my life functional.

One significant thing I have been doing since Edward died is strengthening my faith in God. I spend at least two hours each day contemplating spiritual things.

St. Therese of Lisieux wrote, "See our time of life as what it is: a passage to eternity." Joseph Cardinal Bernadin wrote, "Death is a gift." I know that Edward's death is a passage to his eternal life. I carry a crucifix as a reminder of what Pope Francis said, "... a reminder of the empty tomb, remembering that Jesus died not only to save us from our sins but also to give us eternal life." Many religions, such as Islam, Buddhism, and Hinduism, besides Judaism and Christianity also believe in afterlife. Even if they do not believe in Jesus Christ as the son of God, they believe in God in Heaven.

> **Time**
> There is a time for playing
> Like children going up and down
> The steps.
>
> There is a time For
> feeling sad
> And crying hard—
> Tears like falling rain.
>
> There is a time to dream,
> And realize those dreams
> Like oleanders that finally bloom.

There is a time to grieve,
To love, to laugh, to live,
And to learn—
Let us be someone who
Has lived all his or her time to be.

Whenever thoughts about what happened to Edward upset me, I go outside to garden and to watch the birds, flowers, and butterflies. I also found listening to music soothing and relaxing. The lyrics of some songs touch my soul. I have always loved scents. I burned invigorating scents such as vanilla or orange or eucalyptus candles during my lunch hour, and I used the relaxing scent of ylang-ylang (flowers from a tropical tree) later during the day. I have a Shih Tzu that my daughter gave me after Edward died. I play and spend time with her. Observing her, I learned to enjoy the present moment and live in the present. She barks when she wants something, but otherwise, she is peaceful and contented. I feel relaxed and loving when I am around her.

I spent time with one of my close friends, watch a lot of old movies, cook different recipes, and make new recipes. My other friend, who reads science fiction to relax, shares the stories with me. We also walk in the park or around the building where she works during her lunch breaks. Sometimes I listen to my favorite songs while driving home from work and watch funny old tapes practically every night. I often say to myself, "Take time for yourself each day. Be your own best friend. Have fun and laugh often."

I call or write my friends regularly, and I have one close friend that I talk with almost every day. I also go once a week to visit my grandchildren. I keep writing poetry, continue writing, and read books that help me learn to take good care of myself and my patients.

Stress (One)
Stress affects
Our whole being--
From head to toes,

Internal and external,
Like the polluted air
We breathe.
It can make us indulge
In destructive behaviors,
Causing even more stress.
It can make us sick,
Physically and mentally.

Stress (Two)
What is it about stress?
Isn't life full of stress?
We were born crying
because of stress.
We learn to walk,
keep falling, crying
because of stress.
Eventually, we die
because of stress.

Only the sun, the stars
and the moon
have no stress.

Only when we reach heaven
can stress disappear.
Then perhaps,
we will become the air,
the breeze
that moves the willow trees,
the waterfalls
that continuously
sing.

Types of stress
Good stress is called eustress;
It invigorates us.
Bad stress causes distress;
It can make us ill.

My body
My head hurts.
My tummy hurts.
I have indigestion.
I do not feel well.
I need to see my doctor.
I feel ill.
I need God.

Helpful tips
Rest, adequate sleep, physical exercise,
Diversion, relaxation, massage,
Meditation, music, scents
Can balance our autonomic nervous system
And keep us well—
We are like healthy plants in the sun
playing in the rain
living well.

Stress begets more stress
I have pains in my stomach,
I am nervous and have diarrhea,
I have headaches while I am driving in heavy traffic.
I want to punch
The driver who is driving slow,
I am angry because I am late for work.
I sprain my ankle hurrying up the stairs
I can never win in life—
Life is unbearable
Like a storm.
I am an unripe fig
Falling off the tree.

Make this happen
When we can manage our stress
Each day, our body functions well.
We can live to love—
To realize our reasons for living
Like musicians composing their music.

I also implement the seventeen skill sets I feature in this book on how to live well:

- Altruism (love)—I unconditionally love others as well as myself. I practice kindness and try to bring out the best in others. Ralph Waldo Emerson cited this as one of his criteria for success. He wrote, "Make your environment and the people you interact with happy." Tony Hsieh, author of the book *Delivering Happiness*, made his company Zappos very successful by making the people who work for him happy. I used to be upset when people who worked for me did not do what I wanted them to do. One day, I realized that their ways of looking at things are different from mine. They have a different reality. Once I stopped correcting them and started appreciating the good things that they are doing, I made both them and myself happy.

- Suppression (self-discipline)—I can choose my thoughts, feelings, and activities at any given moment. I can delay gratification, do what I need to do first, and do fun things later. I can do my most important work first and then do relaxing and fun things, such as going to the movies after I do my work. I can discipline myself to think and do constructive things. I am responsible for mastering myself and my environment. I remind myself that "maturity is the ability to postpone gratification" (attributed to Sigmund Freud).

- Anticipation—When I spend some time preparing myself for something painful, such as having to go through a dental procedure, I experience less stress when I eventually have the surgery. I learn to see the advantages and disadvantages of the choices I am making. When I am in a dentist's chair, I can think that this uncomfortable feeling will pass and my teeth will be healthy. I can bear the present discomfort more easily when I can anticipate the future benefits I will gain.

- Sublimation (creativity)—I can channel my painful or socially unacceptable feelings into constructive and creative activities. I find that I can channel and express my painful feelings by writing poetry or gardening. I can write and feel better instead of crying and feeling sorry for myself. Writing this book helped in my healing process. St. Therese of Lisieux wrote from memory and without a rough draft. She created her poetic masterpiece *To Live by Love* shortly before she died. Reading biographies of the saints inspires me to sublimate my emotions.

- Humor—I can laugh at myself. I can see the funny side of things. Often I say to myself: "Laugh—do not take life seriously. Travel through life with laughter in your heart." I remember funny occurrences in my life. I remember this scene: An old couple had the habit of sharing everything. They ordered a meal of a hamburger and French fries. The wife cut the hamburger in half and counted the French fries equally but did not give any to her husband. She then started eating. I was sitting at their next table offered to buy another meal for the husband. The husband smiled and said, "Okay, I will take another meal, and I will give it to my wife. My wife likes to practice her basic math." Norman Cousins was able to become free of his arthritic pains by making himself laugh. He subsequently wrote a book, *Anatomy of an Illness*.

- Faith in God—I have strong faith and trust in God. My faith makes it easier for me to cope with the stresses in my life. I do not think I would be able to handle my life in a mature way if I did not have a strong faith in God. I pray a lot, and no matter how badly I feel, prayers have always helped me feel better. Praying brings me peace, hope, and acceptance in my life. I always feel good when and after I pray. The Swahili in Uganda have a proverb: "Who trusts in God lacks nothing." (*Mwamini Mungu si mtovu*.)

- Acceptance of suffering—Because I accept my suffering as one of the givens in this life, I continue to live fully despite the pain that I am going through in the present moment. I know that it is when we suffer that we grow.

- Peace and joy—I read my prayer books, especially *The Pieta*. I pray the Holy Rosary, contemplate on the Stations of the Cross, and recite the novena to the Infant Jesus of Prague. I also do meditation, focusing on the higher levels of consciousness, and do contemplation. These things bring me peace and joy.

- Self-love and self-esteem—I make sure I do something good for myself each day. Whatever I want in my life, I exert effort and courage to make those needs my priority. I make my dreams come true.

- Courage—Handling life's stress and doing what I am supposed to do requires courage. To gain something, I have to have the courage to do something. I say to myself: "Do not be afraid. Do what you have to do. Confidence is developed one step at a time. Have a brave heart."

- Hope—Because I believe that there is a better day ahead, each day I bear my present burdens easier. I always hope that tomorrow I will have a good day. One of my favorite songs is "Tomorrow." When I am hopeful, I believe that I can master the events that happen in my life. I also have a list of inspiring Filipino songs and popular music that I have memorized and sing. I frequently sing John Lennon's song "Imagine," even though I do not have a good voice. Every morning, as soon as I wake up, I always hope that I will have a good day.

- Work—I know that my stress accumulates when I am lazy and I know most stressful problems do not go away on their own. For instance, it is common sense that I cannot finish correcting this manuscript if I do not continuously work at it. I use the five ego defenses I have been writing about in order to keep me writing. I write because of my love for Edward (altruism). When I am revising this manuscript, I think of how good I will feel when I get this book published and will be able to help many people (anticipation). I lighten up my day, laugh at myself, and make funny comments (humor). I try to be creative in doing my writing. When the tedious thinking and writing upset me, I think of ways to make me feel better, such as cooking or dancing, in between writing (sublimation). I practice self-discipline (suppression) by waking up earlier than usual, so I will have some relaxing time for myself before I continue writing.

- Understanding—The more knowledge and understanding I have about my stressful situation, the better able I am to manage it successfully. I keep learning about truth and life to increase my ability to understand things. I study about our human condition. I know that we live, we suffer, and we die. I live fully and honestly, and I understand that death can happen at any time. Our current technology makes it easier to research and study things. I reflect on my life and apply the wisdom I have learned. I read inspirational books and the Holy Bible.

- Play—After picking up my grandson Zachary from school, we sometimes pass by a toy store just to browse and play with the games displayed on the table. It is a good way for children to relax after school. Sometimes we go to the playground. Zack and my other grandson, Emmett, often play with their friends for an hour after school. Whether I am playing by myself or watching the people I love play, I find these activities to be relaxing and a good form of diversion. I try to have a balanced life of work, love, and play. I enjoy gardening, watching the birds feeding themselves, crocheting, listening to music, talking with my friends, and going places. I love the outdoors: the shore, the parks, the lakes, the ponds, and gardens. I love the arts: museums, exhibits, plays, and concerts. I follow my bliss. A person doesn't need money to do something fun. I know someone who cuts coupons and has fun shopping at the grocery stores using his coupons. He enjoys selling and sells at a flea market. There are so many fun things we can do to enjoy ourselves.

- Happiness—After my office hours, I listen to my favorite music or play with my dog, Chloe; write poems; or go to my backyard and garden. These activities relieve me of stress and make me happy. I also do some hiking. Physical exercise releases endorphins. I choose to be happy and do things that make me happy. I have a notebook of happy occasions and read them once in a while to remind myself to be happy. Happy thoughts create happy feelings. My body responds to my thoughts.

- Energy—I spend my time doing positive things and concentrating on good thoughts. I do not dwell on negative thoughts and feelings. I remind myself that life is short and that I should focus on what I want to be and do. I also reflect on the Ten Commandments to have constructive thoughts, feelings, and actions.

- Handling stress—I have to take good care of myself each day, and spend time handling my life and stress—to have a fulfilling life and at the same time live with manageable stress.

I am adapting to stress
I sing, I laugh, I dance,
I do some physical activities each day,
I imagine the smiles of those I love.

I talk to God,
I ask my favorite saints,
My guardian angels, to guide and help me;
On a sunny day, more so
On a rainy day when the flowers close.

I listen to my favorite music,
I call my friends and laugh.
I work, I write, I meditate, I rest.

I have more energy.
I live to love.
I am alive, productive and well.

I thank God for everything.

CHAPTER 6

─── ❧ ───

Etiology, Anatomy, and Pathophysiology of Stress

An investment in knowledge pays the best interest
—Benjamin Franklin
I am going to discuss the body organs involved
in stress and the abnormal functions of the body
caused by stress. Stress causes a destructive cycle.
When under stress, our whole body suffers,
our coping skills can become less adaptive,
subsequently we develop even more stress.

ETIOLOGY

H ANS SELYE, MD, known as the Father of Stress, defined stress as "any type of nonspecific demand or change made upon our being." There are so many things that cause stress. How we interpret the changes that happen around and within us such as chemical factors, environmental factors, illnesses, relationships, financial problems, and work-related problems are the usual ones. Also, addictions such as overeating, alcohol, or cigarettes; negative thinking; fear; anger; and lack of moral character lead to guilt, worry, avoidable problems, and lower levels of consciousness make one's life more stressful.

At any time in life, we also have day to day things that we consider as stressful and we have to handle them to grow and to stay healthy.

We have an individual ways of responding to stress. Some people get sick easily as a secondary reaction to stress, while others never get sick even when they are exposed to too much stress. Maturity in ego defenses, the intensity and amount of stress, heredity, grace from God, and other individual circumstances all play a part in adapting to stress. Again, learning the seventeen skill sets can influence the way you adapt to stress and live well whatever life brings.

In the January 28, 2013, *American Medical News*, it stated that Americans are the unhealthiest among the seventeen most affluent countries in the world. Our average lifespan is eighty for women and seventy-five for men. The healthiest women are the Japanese with an average lifespan of 85.98 years; for men, the Swiss, with 79.33 years. Obesity rates are cited as one of the factors; and from my experience as an internist, stress is a major factor in overeating and lack of physical exercise, leading to obesity.

When we consider our stresses as challenges, we handle our usual stressful situations constructively.

Martha is transferred to another department at work. She considers her transfer as challenging and exciting. Whereas Joan makes a similar move at her job, but she has been angry at her supervisor for transferring her. She develops pain in her stomach.

Stress can be invigorating when you view the changes as pleasurable and fulfilling. A good support system, harmonious relationships, a job that provides autonomy to express creativity, and no financial worries, go a long way to eliminate a lot of the usual causes of life's stress. Pain and suffering still happen, but they come from other causes. If you have eliminated the common stresses from your life, you will still have others, but will be in a better position to spend your life realizing your potential and helping people. Since it is rather rare to have a life with a good support system or a job that allows for autonomy and creativity, it is important to learn the skills to handle daily stress successfully—which is part of the reason for this book.

ANATOMY

Knowing about your body and how it functions, help you better understand how you feel. Your whole body is governed by your nervous system. The nervous system has two basic components—the central portion (the brain and spinal cord) and the peripheral one (sensory, somatic, and autonomic nervous system).

A person's cognitive mind is based in the brain's two frontal lobes, located behind the forehead. Your right and left frontal lobes mainly determine whether or not the things happening in your life are stressful; whether they are invigorating and relaxing, or are causing you distress.

Annie considers driving to work every morning to be stressful, whereas Jessica finds the same amount of traveling each day to be relaxing. Annie considers staying up late at night as stressful, whereas Jessica can spend sleepless nights without feeling any stress. These differences illustrate that the intensity of your stresses depends on your perceptions.

PATHOPHYSIOLOGY

Personality affects how a person handles stress. I asked a patient, "Why are you crying?" She answered, "I cannot cope with my stress. My apartment has no air conditioner." She used to manage without an air conditioner because she lived without one in the Philippines, but now, because she is living in America, she wants one. She heard that there is a way a physician can write a letter to get her free electricity for an air conditioner.

Another patient came in with a smile and I asked her, "How are you?" She happily answered, "Well, I have a lot of problems at home and with my factory job, but I do my best each day, and I am doing fine. Problems come and go and they do not bother me."

Stress can include positive experiences, such as getting a promotion, going on vacation, getting married, or getting an award. This kind of stress is termed *eustress*. It makes life exciting and invigorating. It brings more life to our lives.

My friend just came back from her adventures in China. She talked about her trip with so much excitement, laughter, and vivacity. The trip added positive things to her life.

Stress can include negative experiences, such as the death of a loved one or being diagnosed with a major illness. This harmful and unpleasant kind of stress is called *distress*.

The intensity and frequency of the changes happening in our lives influence the level of stress we experience. It is therefore constructive to avoid, if possible, too many changes in a short period of time. We need time to adapt to the changes, to reestablish balance.

For example, if you had a broken bone from a car accident, you might postpone changing your job or starting a family right away. You can plan other changes for a much later time.

John and Cora moved to an apartment twice in six months, then bought a new house in another state immediately afterward, fixed their house themselves, and ended up getting into continuous arguments and dissolving their marriage in two years. They both attributed their problems to the distress of having too many problems to cope with continuously since they got married.

On the other hand, Peter and Adriana took their time to enjoy their wedding, visited their relatives and friends, and got to know more about their different ways of handling things after they married. They are happily married and enjoying each other's company. After three years, they decided to start a family.

In general, our social status also influences our stress. Persons in low socio-economic levels usually lack control of their situation. One might have a job where he or she is constantly told what to do, not having any autonomy. We often lack the time to socialize, develop emotional support, or go to the gym if we have to work two or three jobs just to pay bills. If you are in this situation, you will benefit if you make the time to work on your budget, get a better-paying job, work less, and have more time for yourself. If there is no way to change your situation, learning and implementing the seventeen skill sets to become emotionally mature and live well may help you. No matter how hard your life is, if you are doing work for the sake of the family that you love (altruism), you will feel less stress. You will be happy to go to work each day and be able to buy food for your family.

Periodically reflect on your situation; find ways to balance your life; be creative in solving your life situation. When you have time for hobbies, for leisure activities, and to develop a good support system, you handle stress better. People living in poverty in the inner city of Washington, DC, have shorter life spans than those living in affluent conditions in the suburbs. Even if you live in poverty, you can become emotionally mature and live well. You can be creative in finding a better-paying job, or offer your suffering to God, or discipline (suppression) yourself to go to school at night to learn more marketable skills. You can develop your sense of humor and have fun sharing funny stories.

Christopher and Mona conduct a family meeting once a month to plan their activities such as grocery shopping, birthday celebrations, and cleaning their apartment. They are able to implement sublimation (creativity) and anticipation. They anticipate and look forward to having a relaxing vacation once a year.

When our body senses a threat coming from our visual, olfactory, auditory, gustatory, proprioceptive, or tactile sensations, as perceived by our frontal lobes, we experience a stressful event. The brain's frontal lobes (cognitive part) stimulates the limbic system (feeling part). The limbic system in turn, sends messages to the pituitary gland (an endocrine gland that is at the base of our brain). The pituitary gland produces hormones that stimulate the adrenal glands, a pair of glands above the kidneys. (The pituitary gland is called a master gland because it controls other organs such as the adrenals, thyroid, ovaries, and testicles.)

THE ADRENAL GLANDS

The outer part of the adrenal gland is called the *adrenal cortex*, which secretes a hormone called epinephrine, or adrenaline. Epinephrine triggers a series of bodily (fight-or-flight response) changes, including increases in heart rate, blood pressure, and muscle tension, as well as decreases in stomach and intestinal activities. The inner part of the adrenal gland is called the adrenal medulla. It secretes a hormone called glucocorticoid, which affects sugar metabolism and causes a rise in blood sugar. During acute stress, we do not become hungry, and we have more energy. These responses from the hormones coming from the adrenals can be life-saving in an emergency.

Anthony is a firefighter. When called to go to a house fire, he has a lot of energy. He can lift two-hundred-pound objects without any difficulty. He is not hungry, and he can continue working for hours until the fire is controlled.

However, when events such as these happen continuously, as in chronic stress, they affect our peripheral nervous system, nerves that supply the heart, lungs, digestive tracts, genitourinary tracts, lacrimal and salivary glands, reproductive organs, muscles, and skin—practically our whole body.

We have particular weak organs that are more susceptible to certain illnesses when under stress as compared to other organs. Some people develop hypertension, hardening of the arteries (atherosclerosis), heart disease, or stroke; others develop autoimmune diseases, gastritis and peptic ulcer, irritable bowel syndrome, irritation of our urinary bladder, infertility, impotence, or make their diabetes mellitus less controlled.

CARDIOVASCULAR SYSTEM

Stress hormones can cause hardening of the arteries, hypertension, irregular heartbeat, increase the blood's clotting time, increase cholesterol level, and constrict the coronary blood vessels, causing a heart attack.

Luis is suffering from chronic stress at home and at his job. He is hypertensive, diabetic, has occasional heartburn and constipation. Six months ago, he had a heart attack.

Diabetes Mellitus

In acute stress, the body releases hormones such as epinephrine and adrenaline that increase blood sugar. In chronic stress, the body releases glucose from the liver, muscles, and stored fat reserves. This glucose is in addition to what you take in from food, and it makes your blood sugar high. Stress makes diabetes harder to control.

Joseph has been worried about being terminated at work. His blood sugar has been high even though he is maintaining his usual diet.

Gastrointestinal tract

Symptoms such as abdominal cramps, diarrhea, and constipation can be secondary to stress. Raymond suffers from constipation whenever he is extra busy with his work as a school principal. Monica has occasional diarrhea and abdominal cramps whenever she feels stressed out in her job.

The ovaries

Stress inhibits ovulation, thereby causing infertility.

Teresa is a nurse and had a problem conceiving for four years. After she transferred from the intensive care unit to the outpatient clinic, which is less stressful for her, she became pregnant. She now has two healthy children.

THE TESTICLES

Stress also inhibits the testicles from producing testosterone, decreasing male libido.

Working on a shift work schedule, Anthony developed impotence, premature ejaculation, and lack of interest in having sex. His wife suspects that he has another woman, and they argue a lot. Their quarrels add even more stress in their lives.

THE LYMPHATIC SYSTEM

The brain stimulates our immune system, called the *lymphatic system*. Cells in our lymphatic system are called *lymphocytes*. The lymphatic system is composed of lymph nodes, which are found scattered all over our body, in the thymus gland, which is located underneath the middle of our chest bone (sternum), and the bone marrow, which is predominantly found inside our long bones.

When lymphocytes are produced in our thymus gland and lymph nodes, they are called T cells. When lymphocytes originate in our bone marrow, they are called B cells. Diseases that develop because of malfunctions of lymphocytes depend on the origin of the lymphocytes.

Abnormal lymphocytes from the thymus and lymph glands (T cells) make us prone to infection, such as frequent colds, bronchitis, and urinary tract infections. When I work long hours more than usual, my immune system is affected by stress, and I frequently catch a cold.

Abnormal lymphocytes from the bone marrow (B cells) cause autoimmune diseases, such as skin, eye, and nose allergies, rheumatoid arthritis, and multiple sclerosis.

Eleanor has chronic nasal congestion, and her condition flares up whenever she works overtime.

Anna suffers from chronic skin rashes on both legs. She was given a cortisone cream by her dermatologist and was told that her condition was stress-related. She noticed that when she is under a lot of stress, her skin rashes flare up. When she went on vacation to visit her family in South America for three weeks, her rashes almost disappeared.

Juana is twelve years old and had sudden onset of migratory joint pains and swelling for a month. Her blood test confirmed a diagnosis of juvenile rheumatoid arthritis. Her family just moved to another state, and she misses her playmates. Three months ago, her maternal grandmother, who used to live with them and helped raised her, died of a heart attack. She is currently underperforming in school. She is going for art and family therapy, which are helping her pains.

RESPIRATORY SYSTEM

Stress can trigger asthmatic attacks.

Edwin usually has asthma attacks when he is pressured with a deadline for submitting papers for school.

BRAIN FUNCTION

Stress affects us psychologically. It is good to see a psychologist or a psychiatrist to obtain neuropsychological testing and evaluation. The purpose and indications for assessments include the following: to identify cognitive defects; to differentiate depression from psychosis; to follow up and evaluate treatment response; to diagnose learning disorders; and to assess neurotoxic effects, such as substance abuse. Going to see a psychotherapist does not mean that we are "crazy." We have to transcend this misconception.

Our brain is so complex, and many of its conditions need professional evaluation and treatment. The *Diagnostic and Statistical Manual of Mental Disorders* (DMS–V), published in 2013, covers mental health disorders of both children and adults. It is published by the American Psychiatric Association, and provides a common language and standard criteria for the classification of mental disorders. It lists more than 250 mental disorders.

In my clinical practice as an internist and a primary care physician, I see some common stress-related psychiatric problems such as personality disorder, mood disorder (anxiety and depression), and destructive behavior. I think our modern world and modern way of living increase the amount of stress we feel. Although technology is enriching our world, the fast changes are more stressful to live with.

MOOD DISORDER

ANXIETY

When we are worried, afraid, or apprehensive about the future, we can become anxious, causing our blood pressure and heart rate to go up. Sometimes we perspire or are unable to sleep. Sometimes we are aware of the things that make us anxious; at other times we cannot pinpoint the reasons for our anxiety. We may have repressed our thoughts. Psychotherapy, journaling, self-reflection, and intimate conversations can help us become aware of repressed thoughts and traumas.

Claudia knows that she suffers from anxiety. She is afraid to go to unfamiliar places for fear of developing anxiety attacks outside her home. She feels tense and restless. She is irritable and has problems sleeping. She goes to a psychiatrist, a support group, and a Bible study group twice a week, which are helping her.

DEPRESSION

According to the DSM-IV diagnostic criteria for major depressive disorder, at least five symptoms must be present for a period of two weeks and must be a change from the person's previous functioning. Symptoms watched are: depressed mood most of the day; markedly diminished interest or pleasure in all or almost all activities; significant weight loss when not dieting or weight gain; insomnia or hypersomnia most of the day; psychomotor agitation or retardation nearly every day; fatigue or loss of energy most of the day; feelings of worthlessness or excessive or inappropriate guilt; diminished ability to think or concentrate; and recurrent thoughts of death.

Depression statistics show that 5 to 15 percent of office visits to a primary care physician in the US are due to depression. Since depression is more common in women, and I see predominantly women in my practice, I see depression in around 10 to 20 percent of my patients. Once I make a diagnosis of depression, I refer patients to a psychiatrist.

Dysthymia means mild but chronic depression. The word is coined by Dr. Robert Spitzer, an editor of the *American Psychiatric Association's Diagnostic and Statistical Manual of Mental Disorder*. This type of depression can be directly due to a biological chemical imbalance in our brain and can be hereditary.

Mary, her two siblings, and an uncle suffer from depression. Like her diabetes, she was told that depression runs in her family for generations. We should be extra careful to make sure that we do not have too much stress in our lives when depression runs in our family. If it does, pick a career that suits your temperament. Make sure to take good care of your health, and seek consultation with a psychiatrist when you have symptoms of depression.

Clinical depression also impairs cognitive ability, judgment, memory, and concentration. In severe cases, it can cause psychosis. Depression can also cause chronic pain, headache, muscle tension, changes in sleep pattern, and social withdrawal. Depression is called *unipolar* when the signs and symptoms are characteristic only of depression. However, one out of five people who suffer from depression have hypomanic and manic episodes (see the glossary) and are diagnosed with a bipolar disorder. Unipolar depression is more common in women; bipolar affects men and women equally.

Janice has been diagnosed with unipolar depression. She takes psychotropic medications and works as a social worker. She smokes and has a violent relationship with her second husband, but she functions well at work.

Juan is diagnosed with bipolar disorder. When he is manic, he writes nonstop and produces great articles; his work is often published by *The New Yorker*. When he is in a depressed state, he becomes unproductive and does nothing most of the time. Juan has been treated by his psychiatrist for ten years, and his symptoms are stabilized with taking four psychotropic medications.

Anita complained that she was chronically depressed. She is under a psychiatrist's care, goes to group therapy twice a week, and she also attends Al-Anon meetings. She claimed that these programs had helped her, but the medications that her psychiatrist had been giving her help her the most. She also received shock treatments when she first saw her psychiatrist, and her depression was initially intractable.

Depression can be part of what we experience with loss. Since change and loss happen periodically throughout our lifetime, we normally experience the feelings of depression as long as we are living. M. Scott Peck, M.D. wrote, "Depression is normal and a healthy phenomenon. It becomes abnormal or unhealthy only when something interferes with the giving up process with the result that the depression is prolonged and cannot be resolved by completion of the process."

There are developmental stages and bifurcation points in our lives that we have to go through, where we need to grow and change. They cause normal episodes of depression. The changes also cause pain and suffering, which are part of life. There is no joy without pain, and no gain without pain. The bereavement process can manifest itself like a mood disorder, but in bereavement the cause is concrete, and we normally overcome the sad feelings and feel better afterward.

There is a recent magazine called *BP Magazine*. You can access it at http://bipolarmag.com. It is informative, encouraging, and practical reading. It may be helpful for you or for somebody you know who has bipolar or unipolar depression. They also have http://depressionmag.com

Stress depletes our brain's neurotransmitters, such as norepinephrine, serotonin, and dopamine. This is the putative biological cause of depression and the rationale for using prescription drugs, such as sertaline hydrochlorothiazide (Zoloft), paroxetine hydrochloride (Paxil, Pexeva), escitalopram oxalate (Lexapro), bupropion hydrochloride (Wellbutrin), nortryptyline (Elavil), venlafaxine (Effexor), or over-the-counter drugs such as SAM-e and St. John's Wort. These drugs act on the nervous system's neurotransmitters and can restore normal brain function in some people. You need to see a psychiatrist in order to evaluate, treat your condition, and find the medications that you will respond to well. Some people need only one medication; others will need several medications to make them feel better.

Daniel G. Amen, MD, wrote a book entitled *Change Your Brain Change Your Life,* showing brain SPECT (single photon emission computerized tomography). The nuclear medicine test shows pathological pictures of the brain caused by disorders and diseases. He recommends that people suffering from substance abuse have the test done.

Denise has depression that is successfully treated with antidepressants. When she was depressed, she was unemployed. Since she is taking medication, she has a good job and takes good care of herself, her husband, and her school-age daughter.

The limbic system, which is the feeling part in our brain, has a component called the *amygdala*, stimulation of which causes anxiety and fear. Abnormalities in the limbic system will show on the brain SPECT. The amygdala causes anxiety and fear by itself, or it can be triggered by stimuli coming from the frontal cortex (cognitive part).

Judy has been thinking about her upcoming school exam. Her frontal lobes send messages to her amygdala causing her to be anxious.

Mindy feels anxious even when she is not thinking of anything. Her amygdala causes her anxiety by itself.

Antianxiety medications, such as the benzodiazepines: diazepam (Valium) and lorazepam (Ativan) are prescribed to control these symptoms. Antianxiety medications can be habit-forming; antidepressants are not.

The World Health Organization estimated that depression is the fourth leading cause of disability. Also, it is estimated that by the year 2020, depression will be the second most common illness in the US, second only to metabolic syndrome. Understanding stress, accepting pain, loss, and the process of giving up and doing things to prevent and manage our stress can help lower the rates of depression.

INSOMNIA

It is common to develop insomnia as a response to stress. Some people have problems falling asleep; others have problems staying asleep. Maria complains that she is tired all the time because she has a problem falling asleep and lacks sleep. I told her to drink coffee in the morning only, not to lie down unless she is sleepy or planning to sleep, and to use her bedroom for sleeping only—not for other activities such as watching TV, reading, or talking on the phone. Maria was able to sleep regularly after five nights of following my suggestions.

Personality problems

People can develop temporary personality problems secondary to stress. When their stressful situations disappear their personality can become more adaptive.

Dependent

Daniela is twenty-six years old and lived on her own for four years but moved back in with her parents because she was unable to live on her own after she became unemployed. She did not get along well with her parents, but she spent her time worrying about them because, if something were to happen to them, she would have nowhere to go for support. She went back to school and became an occupational therapist. After five years, she got a better-paying job, got her own apartment, and returned to being physically and emotionally independent.

Hostile

Ahmed is constantly angry. He physically abused his two children. He owned a small jewelry store that is being affected by the current economic down-turn. When he used to have money to pay his bills, he enjoyed his kids and had fun going places with them. His personality changed with the stress he is experiencing. He currently has financial, marital, and in-law problems. He told me that the same thing happened to him eight years ago, but he got rid of his anger after his stressful life changed for the better.

Cynical

Terry often makes negative remarks about his coworkers. He had no close friends, he did not like anybody, and nobody liked him either. His cynical attitudes became worse when his supervisor transferred him to a more physically demanding job. He said that his job situation is making him cynical. He said, "I express my stress by taking it out on people."

OBSESSIVE COMPULSIVE

Antonia kept washing her hands, sometimes for five minutes and every hour or so, because she was worried about the germs sticking on her hands. Her obsessive-compulsive behavior started after her husband left her for another woman. Five years after attending the Overeaters Anonymous program and attending a women's support group, her compulsion disappeared. She said that her new friends gave her a sense of belonging and gave her strength to cope with stress.

NARCISSISM

Juan is thirty years old and is a very selfish person. He only thinks of what he can get out of the people around him. He lacks empathy and compassion for anybody. His aunt, who knew him while he was in college, was surprised to find him this way. The stresses he had with his job, his girlfriend, and his recent car accident, causing chronic pain from a herniated disc, made his selfish personality worse. In addition to the stress, he also had many underlying factors that made his personality narcissistic. His personality changed and improved after eight years of psychotherapy and psychoanalysis.

DESTRUCTIVE BEHAVIOR

Stress can lead to destructive behaviors such as smoking, overeating, excessive drinking of alcohol, promiscuity, and indulging in pornography. Even overwork can be destructive, especially if it interferes with other important things such as spending time with our important relationships.

We have problems implementing self-discipline when we are under a lot of stress. Under normal conditions, people can discipline themselves to avoid destructive behaviors, but they can lose their ability to control themselves when they are stressed. Instead, they indulge in activities that temporarily make them feel better but are harmful and can eventually lead to addictions. About two thirds of people monitor their food intake in order to avoid weight gain, but this regulatory behavior is difficult to implement under stress. One successful program to stop overeating is to gradually relearn self-discipline. People are instructed to fast for a day. Once they are able to do that, they are instructed to have only vegetable soup and liquid for two days. Eventually, they are able to discipline themselves to eat balanced meals prescribed to them.

Irene is fifty years old, obese with a bulging abdomen, has diabetes mellitus, hypertension, and a history of two heart bypass surgeries. She knows that the stress she feels from her factory job is causing her to overeat. She has metabolic syndrome. She does not do any physical exercise because she is tired all the time. Metabolic syndrome is a group of diseases, such as type 2 diabetes, mellitus, hypertension, and obesity, associated with concentration of fat in the abdominal area rather than around the hip and buttocks, high LDL (bad cholesterol), low HDL (good cholesterol), increased triglycerides, high blood insulin level, and insulin resistance. People with metabolic syndrome are prone to coronary artery disease, which causes heart attack.

Elbert has taken up destructive behavior in order to cope with his stressful life. He smoked two packs of cigarettes per day and has chronic emphysema. He is on permanent disability for his chronic back problem and spends practically all day watching television. I told him, "How about looking for a part-time job or volunteering at a soup kitchen or going to church?" He said, "No way, I do not want to do any of that." A year later, he was diagnosed with bronchogenic carcinoma, a form of lung cancer, from smoking and he recently died.

PAIN

Sensitivity to pain is enhanced by stress. It is common for people under stress to develop headaches or low back pain. Often pain is a psychosomatic symptom of stress.

Monica had lower back pain that increased in intensity whenever she had an argument with her husband. Her medical evaluation did not reveal a physical cause. Her body produced symptoms triggered by her autonomic nervous system secondary to stress. Through psychotherapy and relaxation, she became pain free.

Nevertheless, pain can be life-saving when it makes us deal with our illness, which can lead to early diagnosis and treatment.

POST-TRAUMATIC STRESS DISORDER

Post-traumatic stress disorder is our response to an overwhelming traumatic event such as the accidental death of a loved one, rape, violent deaths, or war combat. Almost everybody who experiences these feels the trauma. People suffering from post-traumatic stress disorder reexperience the traumatic events, causing fear, horror, helplessness, and avoidance of stimuli associated with the trauma.

Matthew keeps having nightmares and vivid dreams of the Iraq war since he returned home. He was told by his psychiatrist that 3 to 58 percent of people returning from the war suffer from his condition, depending upon what you do in the war, the politics around the war, where it is fought, and the type of enemy you face. He is undergoing behavior therapy, psychotropic medication follow-up, and psychotherapy. He told me that his psychiatrist is very supportive, openly empathetic, and sympathetic to him. Since Matthew enjoys reading and learning things, his psychiatrist recommended several books for him to read, including spiritual books and the Holy Bible. I see him periodically in my office for respiratory ailments, and I have noticed the gradual improvement in his symptoms. He also mentioned that doing meditation daily has helped him live better. He has a supportive girlfriend, an administrative job, and he plays baseball and tennis at least twice a week.

Margoth was diagnosed with post-traumatic stress disorder after she returned from being in the army in Afghanistan. She has been having nightmares and dreams of the bombings that took place years ago. She is under the care of a psychiatrist and a psychologist. Her diagnosis was later changed to bipolar disorder. Lithium has stabilized her mood swings. She goes for individual as well as group therapy. After two years of treatment, she is still taking her medications, but she is working as a secretary and recently got married to a good person she had known for years.

ACUTE STRESS DISORDER

The symptoms of acute stress disorder are similar to post-traumatic stress disorder, but symptoms occur within four weeks of the traumatic event and usually last for two days and no more than four weeks. The intensity of the experience depends upon the severity of the traumatic event.

Edgar suffered from acute stress disorder following a car accident that killed his best friend. Three days after the accident, he felt that things that happened were not real. He had trouble sleeping, had nightmares, and woke up with night sweats and palpitation. His classmates spent a lot of time encouraging him to express his feelings, went hiking with him, and attended concerts to relax. In just three weeks, Edgar felt that he was feeling back to normal.

ABNORMAL BONE METABOLISM—OSTEOPENIA AND OSTEOPOROSIS

Stress affects calcium metabolism in the bone. It can cause osteopenia and osteoporosis. *Osteopenia* means not having enough calcium in our bones. The formation of new bone does not compensate for the bone loss. When osteopenia worsens, it leads to osteoporosis where in bones become fragile and more likely to fracture.

Julia had osteopenia as shown on her bone density test. She was advised to take calcium and eat calcium-rich foods, but she ignored her physician's advice. She went to the emergency room five years later with a hip fracture. This time, her bone density showed osteoporosis in her spine and long bones.

Obviously, her osteopenia worsened and became osteoporosis.

PREMATURE AGING

Stress affects our whole body. It causes aging. I see patients who, in a year's time, aged greatly. Aging, in turn, causes even more stress. Also, our tolerance to stress is diminished with age. Stress triggers a destructive cycle.

GENERAL DISTRESS

Distress is like the potholes that we encounter as we walk through life. Some people can navigate well and grow; others get stuck and live with chronic anxiety and depression; still others get seriously sick or are destroyed.

Maria had many losses in her life. Her parents died when she was a teenager. She moved from state to state almost every year for six years because of her school and financial problems, and yet she managed to finish her college degree, get married, have children, and work in a good job that she loves. She attributed her resilience from her learned optimism growing up, her self-discipline (suppression), her creativity (sublimation) in finding jobs, her sense of humor, and the religious influence of her aunt, who also showed her Saint Paul's letters to the Corinthians. She practiced unconditional love since high school.

On the other hand, Juan also had many loses in his life, but he was not able to cope with his problems. His ego defenses were immature and self-destructive. He dropped out of school and became an alcoholic. I asked him, "Why do you drink?" He said that he is doing it to lessen his anxiety and depression.

Overall effects of stress:

- Decreased productivity
- Decreased enjoyment
- Decreased intimacy
- Less mature coping skills
- Physical and mental illnesses

However, there are other causes besides stress for the conditions listed above. For example:

- Addiction—can be caused by genetic or metabolic vulnerability, secondary to growing up in a dysfunctional family and not being in touch with the "child within," loneliness, lack of strong emotional attachment with family (http://mayoclinic.com, 2013). Also, according to the Mayo Clinic, males are twice as likely as females to have problems with drugs.

- Anxiety—can be caused by taking legal and illicit drugs such as cocaine, corticosteroids, an overactive thyroid gland (hyperthyroidism), and an underactive thyroid gland (hypothyroidism).
- Constipation—can be caused by hypothyroidism, high calcium in the blood (hypercalcemia), Parkinson's disease, low fiber diet, and stroke.
- Colitis—can be caused by infection, radiation, ischemic bowel disease, ulcerative and granulomatous bowel diseases.
- Depression—can be caused by cancer, coronary artery disease, endocrine disorders, fibromyalgia, infection, lupus, nutritional deficiencies, and drugs.
- Dermatitis—can be drug-induced, secondary to heat and sunlight, allergies to inhalants and foods, and infections.
- Diabetes mellitus—a complex group of diseases caused by genetic susceptibility, environmental factors, autoimmune destruction of beta cells, and viruses.
- Hypertension—unknown etiology, genetic susceptibility, kidney disease, and adrenal tumor (pheochromocytoma).
- Heart attack—unknown causes, inflammation of the blood vessels, embolus, high fat diet, low intake of phytochemicals (found in fruits and vegetables), sedentary lifestyle, and tobacco use.
- Impotence—can be caused by endocrine disorders, aging.
- Infertility—can be caused by endocrine disorders, anatomical abnormalities.
- Insomnia—can be caused by withdrawal from psychoactive or antidepressant drugs, hormonal disorders such as hyperthyroidism and menopause, rheumatoid arthritis.
- Obesity—can be caused by genetic predisposition, growing up in a low socio-economic environment, sedentary lifestyle, endocrine disorders, addiction, and metabolic syndrome.

- Osteoporosis—can be secondary to taking corticosteroids, and it is called glucocorticoid induced osteoporosis. Primary osteoporosis is found in women and is termed postmenopausal osteoporosis; above age seventy-five, it is found in both men and women and is termed secondary osteoporosis.
- Personality disorder—there are many types of personality disorders that are not attributed mainly to stress. Causes are varied: developmental problems and growing up in a dysfunctional family are some of them.
- Peptic ulcer—usually caused by bacterial infection (helicobacter pylori), taking nonsteroidal anti-inflammatory medications such as aspirin and ibuprofen. However, stress hinders healing of the ulcer.
- Rheumatoid arthritis—can be caused by genetic predisposition.
- Urinary retention—can be caused by stroke, spine injury.
- Urinary frequency (sometimes called overactive bladder)—can be caused by infection, cystitis, anatomical abnormalities, bladder tumor (http://medicinenet.com, 2013).

CHAPTER 7

✦

Minimize and Manage Stress

> The greatest wealth is health.
> —Virgil

W E NEED A certain amount of stress to live. The right amount of stress motivates us to solve our problems and do more with our lives. It energizes us. Stress and life go together. Total absence of stress is just existing or a psychological stasis, not living.

In life, there are situations where you can learn some things to minimize your stress. There are also proven ways to manage stress.

ASSERTIVENESS

You can be in touch with yourselves and honestly communicate what you want. Abraham Lincoln said that good communication is being honest and kind at the same time. You can share what you want without taking advantage of other people or intentionally harming them.

Anna's friend called her to borrow money. Anna did not tell her that she does not want to lend money. Instead she stopped answering her phone and hoped that her friend would stop calling her. When she finally got the strength to tell her, she felt much better.

Melinda has two teenage children and is going through a divorce. For months she did not tell her children that their father moved in with his girlfriend and filed for a divorce. She felt miserable holding things in and felt much better after she was able to share with them what was going on in her marriage.

SENSE OF CONTROL

When we are young, we tend to make stress go away by asking our parents to help us solve our problems. When we are older, we need to prevent and manage our stress to the best of our ability on our own, so that we live healthy and longer.

There are people who are privileged to have choices in their work. The United States Supreme Court Justices live long lives (University of Minnesota, 2013, http://blog.lib.umn.edu). They have control over their work and probably their personal lives too—they have good income, can choose cases and do the work they love. They can change history, and they can work as long as they want; they have no mandatory retirement age.

People living in nursing homes who are given some control, autonomy, and an outlet to express themselves, live longer than people who do not have these options. One nursing home I frequently visit has their residents' own plants at their bedside. Residents are also told that they can take their sleeping pills whenever they want to, and they are encouraged to participate in arts and crafts, but only if they want to. Some of them have lived there for the past twenty years without having to go to the hospital.

I have three patients in their nineties who are healthy and living independently. They live simple lives. Two engage in volunteer work and spend their time doing other activities they enjoy. They solve their own problems whenever they occur. They control and manage their lives with their positive attitude toward things.

Studies with musicians show that those playing in a chamber music group have less stress than those playing in an orchestra.

Musicians playing in chamber music groups have more freedom with their schedule, whereas those playing in an orchestra have more rules to comply with the conductor's demands.

PREDICTABILITY

In general, when you are making the policies, you have less stress than when you are told what to do, unless you have a passive personality type. Therefore, it is wise to get a job suited for you. The National Institute of Occupational Safety and Health compiled a list of occupations that are the most and the least susceptible to stress-related diseases. For example, some of the occupations most susceptible to stress are: secretary, laborer, and machine operator; and some of the least susceptible are: craftsmen, warehouse checkers, college professors, and child-care workers.

CULTIVATE SUPPORTIVE AND INTIMATE RELATIONSHIPS

Family and friends who can support us in our time of need are very important in diminishing our stress. They can mitigate our grief and pain.

Cultivate and have an ongoing relationship with a good support system. In my experience, you need at least three intimate friends to share the good and bad times of your life. The more intimate friends you have, the better and richer your life is. There are different types of problems in life, and you can usually get specific and special wisdom from one certain friend more than another. If I am having work-related problems, I discuss them with one particular close friend; if I am having personal problems, I talked them over with another friend.

It is practical and your life is richer when you have friends in various age groups and in different types of work. George E.

Vaillant, MD, wrote, "Like art, intimacy is an act of creation, but intimacy far surpasses art as a cure for emotional suffering."

Avoid saying negative things, especially to your family and friends. They resent negativity from us more than strangers do. Appreciate, approve, and accept people. Praise and encourage good behavior. Read Dale Carnegie's classic book *How to Win Friends and Influence People*. Our usual day-to-day problems involve our relationships. If we have no problems with our relationships, then we have less stress. Be nice. "Earn thy neighbor's love." Life is short, be nice!

Modifying type A, B, C, and D personalities

Definitions of *personality types* came into existence through research

There are four personality types.

People with type A personalities are impatient, hurried, very competitive, and hostile. These characteristics lead to hypertension and coronary heart disease. A friend told me that I have a type A personality, and I agreed because I am sometimes impatient and I focus on things I want to do. I read the description of the type A personality, and in reality I do not have the characteristics described except that I am usually on time and I hurry when I am late. I am seldom angry and I am not hostile. The only thing that makes me a type A personality is that I am punctual and conscious of time. People who have type A personalities are highly independent and always looking for ways to improve or find solutions to problems. They are usually good leaders.

People with type B personalities are laid-back and easygoing, but like to be in the limelight. They are good in sales. They handle rejection well. They have low stress levels because of their personality. Nothing bothers them. The disadvantage is that they tend to procrastinate.

People with type C personalities hold their emotions in. They are introverted, very cautious, prone to depression, and reserved. Some believe that this personality is cancer-prone, although this belief is still controversial.

People with type D personalities type resist change and are not adventurous. They are pessimistic. Ellen told me that she lives a miserable life. She does not like her job but keeps her job. She thinks she cannot find another job. She works because she worries about not having money to pay her credit cards. She has diarrhea on and off, especially when she has a lot to do, and she thinks that eventually she will have cancer. She actually was just diagnosed with heart disease and cancer (http://www.oncologypractice. com 2012).

There is another personality test, the Myers-Briggs personality test, that schools use to help guide students choose their careers. Personality characteristics also help us understand people.

Although we have a basic personality type, usually we have combinations of different personality characteristics. We can learn to change ourselves, be flexible, and grow. We can continue to adapt and express who we truly are, to live our truth, yet learn to be flexible and change to improve ourselves. I am learning to be more laid back, and to acquire more characteristics of a type B personality by talking to myself and saying, "Take your time. Tomorrow is okay, too." I consciously correct myself when I want things done as scheduled. It is working.

TIME MANAGEMENT

It is productive to spend our prime time doing what we want to accomplish in our life. We delegate to others what others are better able to do. We can do things we need to do, and we try not to procrastinate. The *Pareto principle* indicates that 20 percent of the things that we do create 80 percent of the results that are beneficial. It is wise to follow this rule in managing our time and activities. Business consultant Joseph M. Juran suggested the principle named after the Italian economist Vilfredo Pareto, who observed that 20 percent of the pea pods in his garden contained 80 percent of the peas.

We can categorize activities and address them as follows:

- Important but not urgent
  For example, aerobic exercise for twenty minutes; progressive relaxation
- Important and urgent
  For example, renewing a soon-to-expire driver's license
- Unimportant and not urgent
  For example, rearranging a clothes closet
- Unimportant but urgent
  For example, fixing a leaky faucet

We can avoid stress by not spending our energy solving urgent problems unnecessarily. We accomplish more when we do important things, especially during our prime time.

NUTRITION

Here are some guidelines to healthy eating:

- Eat a variety of foods. Make your plate colorful and beautiful.
- Eat a balanced meal, with 60 percent carbohydrate, 20 percent protein, and 20 percent fat.
- Eat starch and fiber. Make about half of your plate vegetables and fruits.
- Eat lean meat, fish, legumes, and dairy products for protein. Drink 1 or 2 percent fat content milk or soy milk. Ideally, eat meat to flavor dishes, not a big portion by itself. This

will avoid eating a lot of toxic chemicals from meat, which contains nitrates and synthetic growth hormones such as zeranol, trenbolone acetate, progesterone, and testosterone.

- Avoid sweets, fructose, and diet and sugary drinks. Drink water instead.
- Avoid too much salt. Eat less than 2400 mg per day. Compare sodium content of foods.
- Limit your intake of fat, cholesterol, saturated fats, and foods containing trans-fatty acids.
- Drink alcohol in moderation. You may drink a glass of red wine with your dinner.
- Avoid artificial coloring and additives.
- Schedule your meals at usual times as much as possible. Notice how you feel when you are full and when you are hungry. You do not need to eat when you are not hungry unless it is your scheduled time to have your meals.
- Drink a lot of clean water (six to eight glasses per day), preferably before meals.
- Take a daily multivitamin supplement.

Balance your caloric intake with your daily caloric expenditures. It takes 3500 kcal (calories) to lose a pound of body fat. If you want to lose weight, aim at losing about one pound per week by lowering your calorie intake by roughly 3500 kcal per week or increasing your physical activity to burn around 500 kcal per day (500 kcal x 7 days = 3500 kcal deficit per week). This is losing one pound of fat per week, assuming that you are eating balanced meals and have enough protein in your diet. When you are lowering your caloric intake or exercising more to have a deficit of 3500 kcal per week and your weight fluctuates as much as two to four pounds from day to day, the change in your weight is usually due to fluid loss or retention.

Try not to overeat. Eat about 500 calories per meal and eat four to five times a day if you are physically very active and require more calories for the day. Carbohydrates and proteins have four calories per gram, fats have higher calories—nine calories per gram. Many boxed and canned foods have the number of calories listed on their labels. Familiarize yourself with the foods you frequently buy. Note that the calories are listed per serving, not for the total container. For nutrients, fresh produce, especially organic produce, retain their nutrients best. Second are frozen foods, and the least nutritious are canned foods. Even if canned foods are less nutritious than fresh produce, you can still eat them if you prefer them and they are more practical for the recipe you are making. Be flexible. Do not eat canned foods all the time.

Here are over thirty foods that have known nutritional and medicinal merit. Some produce and restore the neurotransmitters in our nervous system; others improve our mood, increase our tolerance to pain, and help our immune system: salmon; green tea; olive oil; coconut oil; cherries; blueberries; whole grains such as oats, corn, and barley; mango; banana; oranges; avocado; mangosteen; pomegranate; butter; sweet potatoes; sesame seeds; flaxseeds; soy bean; wheat germ; brussels sprouts; kale; broccoli; cabbage; carrots; coffee; garlic; ginger; lemon; onions; parsley; peppermint; and watercress. Hippocrates wrote, "Food is medicine."

If you have specific medical conditions such as diabetes, gout, gluten sensitivity, or kidney stones, ask your physician to give you a list of foods that you should avoid and foods you can have.

PHYSICAL EXERCISE

There are three types of physical exercise:

- Aerobic exercise using heart and lungs
- Stretching for flexibility of joints and body
- Strengthening muscles, such as weight lifting and resistance training

All of these exercises are important to keep fit, but the most important is aerobic exercise. There is strong evidence that aerobic exercise helps prevent Alzheimer's disease and prevent cardiovascular diseases (http://sciencedaily.com, 2012). I am doing more physical activities myself because I want to get rid of the arthritic pain in my left knee. The endorphins produced by doing physical exercises help ease my pain and also increases my sense of well-being.

Breathing balances our autonomic nervous system and directly relieves us of stress. It also stimulates our lymphatic system and improves our immunity. We should aim at doing aerobic exercises thirty minutes three times a week (ninety minutes total). We can do activities such as brisk walking, gardening, or housework continuously for at least thirty minutes at a time. Consult your physician before starting any strenuous physical exercise, especially if you have lived a sedentary lifestyle.

Here is a formula for challenging your cardiovascular system by increasing your heart rate. (Take 220 subtract your age and then multiply by 70 percent, for optimal and target heart rate.) For example, if you are 50 years old, $220 - 50 = 170$. Seventy percent of 170 is 119 beats per minute. A good guideline to follow is that you should be able to talk while doing strenuous aerobic exercise. Aerobic exercise is physical exercise of relatively varied intensity that depends primarily on the aerobic generating process. Aerobic literally means "living in air." Examples are running, swimming, cycling, and walking. Dr. Kenneth Cooper did extensive research in 1960 on over five thousand air force personnel. He recommended that the intensity of aerobic exercise should be between 60 to 85 percent of maximum heart rate.

Do about two to three minutes of stretching exercises to warm up and to cool down. You can count your heart rate by feeling your pulse in your wrist, carotid artery (the side of your neck) or apex of your heart (left front chest). Whenever possible, move around; do not live a sedentary life.

Potential benefits of regular exercise include:

- increased stamina
- better sleep
- improved mood
- greater ability to concentrate
- improved brain function
- prevention of Alzheimer's disease
- better control of body weight
- increased energy
- decreased anxiety, anger, and hostility
- lower risk of stroke and heart attack
- improved immune response
- pain relief by the release of endorphins in the nervous system
- relief from stress

OUTLET FOR FRUSTRATION

There are times when things do not go the way we want. There are times when we do not get what we want. Have a hobby you enjoy. You need to have some outlet: physical activities you enjoy such as dancing and gardening, going to the movies, window-shopping, doing arts and crafts, or reading, to get rid of frustrations and feel better. You can also express your frustrations through journaling.

MUSIC

Music is food for the body and soul. Listen to your favorite music or play a musical instrument. Make music a part of your life. Music is a universal language. Steve Jobs thought about the popularity of music and invented iTunes. Music, like art, is use for therapy.

Many years ago, my daughter Melin, with my son Edward's help, started a nonprofit organization called Music for Healing. One of their T-shirts had Aaron Copland's quote, "No one ever regretted being a musician."

RELAXATION

- One quick way to relax is progressive relaxation. Tighten your whole body, starting with your face, down to your toes; then limber your whole body and relax. Whenever you remember, check your body, if it is tense, do progressive relaxation.
- Do activities that you enjoy, such as singing, dancing, playing, gardening, or cooking. These activities relax your mind and body. You can plan a relaxing vacation or activities regularly as diversion from your stressful life. You can also learn t'ai chi, qigong, yoga, and Reiki. Get a massage. Try body, head, foot, and hand massages. One of my friends gives me gift certificates around my birthday for spa treatments.
- Use scents. Examples of relaxing scents are: lavender, ylang-ylang, and chamomile. Invigorating scents are lemon grass, jasmine, peppermint, and eucalyptus. I picked my favorite scents by smelling a variety of flowers, fruits, and leaves. Take a leisurely day. Go to a garden or a holistic health shop and identify your favorite scents. I love scents. I use them depending on what I feel at the moment. When I need to relax, I use relaxing scents. When I need to have more energy, I use invigorating scents. One of my patients got rid of her insomnia by using ylang-ylang (a tropical flower from a flowering tree) one hour before her sleeping schedule.

- Spend time down at the shore, mountains, by waterfalls, or in sunny areas. Negative ions are odorless, tasteless, and invisible molecules that we inhale in these environments. Some people believe that once these ions reach our bloodstream, they produce biochemical reactions that increase the levels of serotonin, a neurotransmitter that improves our mood, boosts our energy, and increases our sense of well-being. People who are fortunate to live by the seashore, the mountains, or by waterfalls notice the difference in how they feel when they are living around them compared to being away from this environment. Pierce J. Howard, PhD, wrote in *The Owners Manual for the Brain* that negative ions increase the oxygen's brain blood flow resulting in higher alertness and more mental energy.

- Seek a beautiful environment. Take a hike in the park, by the pond, by the lake, or in the mountains. Surround yourself with beauty. Have flowers and plants in your home. Make your home beautiful and relaxing. Hang beautiful pictures in the rooms where you spend much of your time. Spend time looking at beautiful pictures in your albums and books.

- Own a pet. My Shih Tzu is the best gift my daughter has given me.

- Expose yourself in the sun for twenty to thirty minutes each day. Stay under a bright light for five or ten minutes without wearing sunglasses. Sunshine stimulates our brain, energizes us, and prevents depression. I have an ultraviolet light I use in my bedroom. People living in Scandinavian countries who live without sunshine for months suffer from depression. If you stay in the sun for more than ten minutes a day, wear your sunglasses to prevent cataracts.

PRACTICE MEDITATION

Meditation makes us happy and positive. It makes our mind calm and peaceful. We can practice meditation by doing abdominal breathing for twenty minutes twice a day (forty minutes total). There are many ways to meditate, such as: mindfulness meditation, progressive relaxation, yoga, or just concentrate on your breathing. Meditation brings a greater sense of well-being, greater concentration, enables more energy, and puts us in touch with our soul. The alpha brain waves elicited by meditation integrate the right and left side of our brain. Yoga is a system of exercises that uses our will to control our mind and body. It improves our sense of well-being while stretching muscles and joints.

INSTRUCTION ON HOW TO MEDITATE TO RELIEVE STRESS

Sit in a comfortable position. Take a deep breath. Inhale through your nose, feeling the air filling the lower parts of your lungs and expanding your abdomen. Then breathe out through your mouth as slow and long as comfortable. When exhaling say to yourself, "I am calm and relaxed." You can count up to four when you breathe in, hold your breath and count seven, and exhale with a count of eight. Once you have done this several times, you do not have to count, just inhale deeply and exhale longer than you inhale. Inspiration stimulates our sympathetic nervous system and expiration stimulates our parasympathetic nervous system. Parasympathetic nervous system stimulation causes relaxation, so that exhaling slowly relaxes you.

HOW TO HAVE MORE ENERGY

When you feel that you are sluggish and need more energy, you can inhale deeply to stimulate your sympathetic nervous system and release adrenaline. You can make your inhalation and exhalation about equal duration.

SLEEP

Get adequate sleep every day. Most people need seven to eight hours of sleep every twenty-four hours to function at an optimal level. Adequate sleep prevents depression and maintains good brain function such as our memory. Some people need a little more and some need less. It is also good to follow a scheduled sleeping time. My routine is to go to sleep early in the evening and wake up early in the morning. If your job involves shift work, try to negotiate to keep the same schedule so that your body will not be stressed from changing your sleeping time schedule.

STRESS INOCULATION

If we are exposed to managing stress a little at a time, we become emotionally stronger and are better able to handle future stressful situations. We develop higher frustration tolerance and endurance. When I was working as a medical intern, I was continuously called to handle all the medical problems in one unit. I found the work to be very stressful. But after several months, I got used to it and the busy work did not bother me any longer. Be patient with yourself. The intensity of some stressful situations diminishes after a while.

John initially found his 4:00 a.m. job to be very stressful. He had a hard time waking up early in the morning. After a month, he got used to waking up early and found waking up early to be less stressful.

COGNITIVE RESTRUCTURING

Focus periodically on relaxing things, learn to see the silver lining in every situation. We can also practice *rational emotive therapy* (RET). Albert Ellis, PhD, became a famous psychotherapist and lived into his nineties teaching RET. If you are not happy, then you can dispute your thinking to make yourself feel better. His motto was: "Be kind to yourself and do not hurt others." He and Dr. Irving Becker wrote the book *A Guide to Personal Happiness*, in which they implement rational emotive therapy.

Having a positive mental attitude is another form of cognitive restructuring. Make a habit of looking for the advantages of every disadvantage. Avoid negative thinking.

It is normal to wonder what other people think about you when you are below twenty years old. When you are forty years old, you learn to think about yourself. When you are sixty years old, you realize that people never think about you. They think only about themselves. Knowing this can eliminate energy wasted because of not being self-reliant, especially once you are over forty years old. David Foster Wallace wrote," You'd be a lot less concerned about what others think of you if you knew how rarely they do."

TRANSFORM STRESS BY CONCENTRATING ON LOVE

Love releases endorphins, a natural opiate-like neurotransmitter that makes us feel good. Put your hands over your heart. Do abdominal breathing, focusing on the love that you have for another person, such as your grandchild. Do this for twenty minutes. Then also do the same breathing exercises focusing on the love you have for yourself.

FOCUS ON A HIGHER LEVEL OF CONSCIOUSNESS

Unconditional love, understanding, compassion, peace, and joy enhance our well-being and enable us to live more fully. Apathy, shame, guilt, grief, desire, and fear lower our energy level and make our life more stressful. Try to be a good person. Cultivate good values.

STRENGTHEN YOUR SPIRITUALITY

Live to give and serve others. Live a prayerful life. People who are very religious and pray a lot are healthier and live longer (http://huffingtonpost.com, 2011). Robert Sapolsky wrote in his book *Stress and Your Body* that religious beliefs tend to increase protection against cardiovascular disease and increase life expectancy.

When I used to see patients at a nursing home, I took care of a patient who spent many hours every day saying the rosary. She lived to be 101 years old.

Prayers bring peace of mind and confidence that things happen for a good reason or that things will get better. We live with altruism and asceticism by offering our sufferings to God. Praying is also a form of meditation; it relaxes our mind and body. We also rest and sleep better after praying.

However, being spiritual does not necessarily mean living longer. Some saints died very young. There are other factors governing our longevity such as our heredity, environment, and God's will.

A prayer can be a direct conversation with God; a plea on behalf of someone or yourself; a time of adoration and thanksgiving; a quiet time of contemplation; a period of listening to what God tells you; and a time to receive God's love.

Reflect on some excerpts from the Bible, also prayers and religious teachings that I included in Appendixes B and C.

Implement the seventeen skill sets in this book on how to live well whatever life brings. Refer to Appendix A.

Some outcomes of good adaptation to stress include:

- increased self-love, self-esteem, self-respect, and self-confidence
- improved physical health
- resistance to illness such as infection, autoimmune diseases, and cancer
- improved mental health (love and work)
- resistance to future stress
- feeling good, productive and well
- effective in solving problem

Janice used to have migraine headaches and lacked the energy to do the things she loved to do. I gave her a copy of this section on how to manage stress. After following my suggestions faithfully for a month, she noticed that her headaches were less frequent, and she had a better sense of well-being.

After learning ways to minimize and manage stress, we need to use what we have learned and apply them in our life by using discipline.

CHAPTER 8

Discipline

Without discipline we can solve nothing.
—M. Scott Peck, MD

C HAPTER 1, ON mature ego defenses, mentions self-discipline or suppression, but here is a whole chapter about self-discipline, which is the key to success in applying what we have learned—doing what we need to do each day, changing some unhealthy habits, solving our problems, and growing.

Jessica knows that she has to find a better-paying job, but she has so many excuses and has so many reasons for not actively looking for one. She said, "I do not want to commute, I do not want to wake up very early, and I do not want to learn the computer." Instead, she keeps her two-hour-per-day job as a cashier, spends every afternoon watching her soap operas, and goes shopping whenever her husband can spare their car for her use. She is sixty-pounds overweight, but she does hardly any physical exercise, nor does she follow a healthy diet because she hates doing both.

Having discipline means enduring the discomfort of doing what we need to do first and learning to delay gratification. It means developing a good work ethic. It also means taking responsibility for ourselves and our lives. Problems do not go away on their own. We have to take the responsibility for solving them. Learning discipline starts when we are young. It is harder to learn it as adults, but we can still do it. Learning is a lifelong process. If you used to be self-disciplined when you were younger, but have difficulty being so now, you are probably under a lot of stress, and the stress is causing you to become less emotionally mature—using less mature ego defenses.

Cynthia is a morning person and has a daily to-do list. She schedules the important and hardest things to do in the morning. Once she is done with her difficult work, she enjoys her leisurely afternoons even more. In high school she learned from her aunt that we are responsible for our own life, and that problems are part of life. Realizing this truth early in life gave her a good foundation. Whatever she wanted in life, she worked hard to earn it. Cynthia borrowed CD tapes and nonfiction books every summer in between her college years. Her favorite books are *The Road Less Traveled*, by M. Scott Peck, MD, and *The Power of Positive Thinking*, by Norman Vincent Peale. She also reads a lot of classic literature, spiritual and philosophy books. She said to me, "Knowing the truth about life and accepting our human condition are very important to me. These are things I live by."

Self-discipline becomes easier with practice. People learning martial arts, musical instruments, or sports can master themselves more easily than people who never had the experience of pursuing activities that require discipline and hard work.

Manuel attributed his success in college to how disciplined he had always been in practicing the piano practically every day since grade school.

We discipline ourselves because we love ourselves. Loving oneself requires effort and courage. We sacrifice and delay gratification, and do the things we need to do to help ourselves because we have self-respect. It is hard work and painful at the time we are doing them, but we have to live through the pain and night to come out on the pleasant and bright side of our life later on. If we are lazy and fearful to do things, we cannot solve our problems or improve ourselves and our lives.

Since stress lowers our ability to practice self-discipline, we need to prevent unnecessary stress and handle our everyday stress.

Some things we need to do daily and make them routine. Do these important but not urgent activities daily:

- Aerobic physical exercise—continuous walking or physical work for at least twenty minutes daily.
- Deep abdominal breathing—twenty minutes daily, ideally twice per day. Abdominal breathing balances your autonomic nervous system and relaxes your body.
- Develop a positive mental attitude habit; avoid negative thinking.
- Have an ongoing relationship with God, yourself, and your intimate friends—make these important in your life.
- Eat properly and nutritiously.
- Get adequate rest and sleep.
- Manage your time with flexibility and balance while minimizing and handling your stress.
- Remember what you live for, and live truly for yourself. Here are the twelve "riches of life" from Napoleon Hill's book, *You Can Work Your Own Miracles*
    - Positive mental attitude
    - Sound physical health
    - Harmony in human relation
    - Freedom from fear
    - The hope of future achievement
    - The capacity for faith
    - Willingness to share one's blessings
    - A labor of love
    - An open mind to all subjects
    - Self-discipline
    - The capacity to understand people
    - Economic security
- Reward yourself for your hard work
- Make time to play.
- Be your own best friend.

- Engage in activities that nourish your soul.
- Learn something and grow each day.

In 1958, Marie Jahoda, a professor of social psychology at Sussex University, identified characteristics that she found to be present in people who were considered normal. Known as Ideal Mental Health, these are:

- efficient self-perception
- realistic self-esteem and acceptance
- voluntary control of behavior
- true perception of the world
- sustaining relationships and giving affection
- self-direction and productivity

Voluntary control of behavior means self-discipline. Also, all these characteristics considered to be components of positive mental health are useful in implementing self-discipline.

Examples of persons as described by Marie Jahoda

Jennifer is twenty years old and knows what she wants as far as career and the kind of husband she wants (efficient self-perception). She has a loving family, some close friends, and she lives a balanced life (loving relationships). She goes to school full time and has a four-hour five-day-a-week part-time job. She spends time with her friends on Saturdays and teaches Sunday school (self-direction and productivity). She enjoys going to concerts and hiking. She knows what she can do and accepts her limitations (realistic self-esteem and acceptance). She watches what she eats and goes to the gym three times a week (self-discipline). She lives an ordinary good life with manageable stress. She is a happy person and has close friendships with three people around her age.

Oliver is forty years old, a successful businessman who has close friends, accepts and is aware of his limitations, and is emotionally and physically self-reliant. Now that he has a stable business (which he had worked hard for in the last ten years), he dates people, hoping to find a suitable partner in life. He wants to raise children and currently volunteers for Big Brothers and Big Sisters.

Self-discipline is basically controlling your mind to do what you want. It is choosing what you want to do that is beneficial for yourself, and having the patience and perseverance to do that. A common proverb says, "If there is a will, there is a way." It takes a will to decide what to do, and the effort and courage or self-love to do it. You sacrifice for the present in order to get rewards later on.

Use self-discipline to focus your thoughts on higher levels of consciousness, follow the Ten Commandments, or be a good and loving person. The word *discipline* is derived from the word *disciple*. We can have Jesus Christ, Buddha, Krisna, or Muhammad as our role models for living.

Occasionally, I practice my three-day mental diet. For three days I will not think or say anything negative or useless. I repeat the AA serenity prayer when necessary. For example, whenever I think back and wish Edward were still alive, I do these things primarily to master my thoughts and to use my time constructively instead of rethinking unproductive thoughts. After I am successful doing this for three days, I increase my goal to doing it for five days, and then for seven days. Discipline becomes easier with practice. Try it with what you want to do!

Many people know what they want in their lives, but they are unfulfilled because they lack discipline. They procrastinate in doing things they need to do and they are lazy. They need to learn discipline to change so that their lives will be better.

Here are some ways to develop self-discipline or make it easier to do:

- fasting
- positive affirmation or self-suggestion
- visualization or imagining
- anchoring
- neuro-associative conditioning
- yoga
- prayers
- making a promise
- meditation
- AA's serenity prayer
- the seventeen skill sets described in this book
- role models
- making a checklist

FASTING

Fasting is a common way to practice self-discipline. Religious rules make people fast as a way of sacrifice. Orthodox Jews observe fasting from sunrise to sunset on many of their holidays throughout the year. Muslims observe fasting daily for a month during Ramadan—the ninth month of the Muslim calendar year. Devout Catholics give up meat during lent and other holy days of obligation. When I was growing up in the Philippines, I used to fast from midnight until after I received the Holy Eucharist in the morning.

POSITIVE AFFIRMATION OR SELF-SUGGESTION

Whatever goals you want to realize in your life, write them down as if they are happening already.

Example of my daily affirmation:

- I feel good today. I can do whatever I have to do.
- Today is a good day. I will do the difficult things first.
- It is okay to live with pain and suffering.
- I am flexible and love unconditionally.
- I live with peace and joy.

Emile Coue, a French physician, had this popular self-suggestion, "Every day and every way I am getting better and better." When I was just starting my practice, one of my patients used to use Dr. Coue's words as her daily mantra. She lived to ninety-four. She suffered degenerative arthritis for thirty-four years. She lived with minimal pain by practicing self-suggestion four times a day. The days when her pains were severe, she did self-suggestion every hour until she fell asleep. Self-suggestion is another term for self-hypnosis.

VISUALIZATION WITH POSITIVE EMOTIONS

Imagine your affirmations as if they are happening at the present moment, and feel the positive emotions accompanying the activities.

For example:

- I see myself enjoying eating fruits and vegetables and savoring the taste, the smell, and the beautiful and colorful arrangement on my plates.
- I imagine myself doing and enjoying my physical exercises.

ANCHORING

Remember your affirmations and visualizations and touch one of your fingers to anchor these constructive feelings and thoughts. Make a habit of remembering them until you can automatically recall and feel the good feelings just by touching the fingers where you anchored them.

Whenever I remember happy occasions with my two grandsons, I made a habit of touching my index fingers. I have been doing this for four years. After a year of doing it, I noticed that I always feel happy when I touch my index fingers. I call my index fingers my *happy deposit box*.

This phenomenon is an application of Ivan Pavlov's experiment with dogs. Pavlov rang the bell, gave food to the dog, and noticed that the dog salivated. Later, whenever he rang the bell, the dog automatically salivated, even without the food. I have also anchored my good feelings on my right knee after doing my aerobic exercises. Whenever I touch my right knee, I remember feeling good.

NEURO-ASSOCIATIVE CONDITIONING

Associate the things that are good for you with *happy feelings* and the things that are not good for you with *unhappy feelings*. Likewise, will yourself to think, want, and do the things that are good for you, and associate them with good feelings. Change your association to pleasure and pain. For example, make physical exercise pleasurable and being lazy not pleasurable.

I wanted to be able to play my favorite music pieces, but sometimes I did not feel like practicing. Once I associated practicing the piano as being pleasurable and procrastinating practice as not pleasurable, practicing the piano became pleasurable.

YOGA

There are many ways of doing yoga. You can do yoga with the intensity and difficulty commensurate with your physical condition. Ask your own physician for recommendations. The basic principle is to use your mind to control your emotion and your body. Yoga is a good tool for practicing discipline.

PRAYERS

Prayers bring peace, acceptance, and confidence. Make your own prayers to God. Ask God to help you develop discipline in whatever you want to achieve. Contemplate and listen to what God wants you to do.

MAKING A PROMISE

If you promise yourself to reward yourself after you have done something difficult, this usually enhances your ability to discipline yourself. If you are religious, you can promise God that you will discipline yourself, and you will have more motivation to do so.

MEDITATION

People often practice meditation to reduce stress. It is a way to practice self-discipline, self-knowledge, and improve our ability to be calm, productive, and feel better. We have more self-discipline when we practice meditation regularly.

AA PROGRAM

There are at least three hundred programs patterned after the Alcoholics Anonymous program. Overeaters Anonymous, Co-Dependents Anonymous, and Gamblers Anonymous are some examples.

Friedrich Oetinger(1702-1782) and Reinhold Niebuhr (1776-1831) wrote this AA serenity prayer: "God, grant me the SERENITY to accept the things I cannot change, COURAGE to change the things I can, and WISDOM to know the difference. Living one day at a time, enjoying one moment at a time, accepting hardships as the pathway to peace, taking, as Jesus did, this sinful world as it is, not as I would want it. Trusting that You [God] would make all things right if I surrender to Your [God's] will so that I may be reasonably happy in this life and supremely happy with You [God] forever in the next. Amen."(There are many variations of the wording of this prayer and discussions about who really are the authors)

The successful Alcoholic Anonymous program was founded by Bill Wilson. He wrote a letter to C. G. Jung (six months before Jung died at age eighty-six), thanking him for curing his alcoholism. Wilson had gone to Zurich to seek treatment for his condition, and Jung told him, "There is nothing I can do for you. You have a spiritual disease." His realization of his spiritual deficiency led to his developing the twelve-step program of Alcoholics Anonymous. (See Appendix B.)

The first three steps are about acknowledging that we need God in our life. Steps four to nine are about complete evaluation, accounting, cleaning up our wrongdoings, and repentance. Steps ten to twelve are about our daily acknowledgement of our sins, repentance, and a resolve to change and keep ourselves clean.

A patient showed me his silver cross with the twelve steps inscribed on it. He reads them several times a day. He has been sober for the past thirteen years. He is an inspiration to others in the meetings he attends by sharing his testimonials.

Role Models

Have role models. For example, Gwyneth Paltrow, interviewed on *Good Morning America* in September 2013, was asked for the reason for her success and beauty. She said, "Very hard work and discipline." We can have role models like her.

Make a Checklist

Write on it whatever you need to do that is important to you. Build your habit by writing things down and checking them off after you do them. List and live a balanced life of work, love, and play.

Here is an example of how to use the seventeen skill sets to lose or maintain weight.

1. Altruism or love—Eat healthy, balanced meals because you want to be healthy as a way of loving yourself. You do not want to be sick and become a burden to those you love.
2. Suppression or self-discipline—If you are overweight, make losing weight one of your goals in life. Do not overeat in the present and regret that you overate later.
3. Anticipation—If you do not solve your weight problem now, it will become even harder to do it later on. Reward yourself after losing the weight you plan to lose. Put money away every week while losing weight and use the funds to go on vacation in the future.
4. Sublimation or creativity—Be creative in managing your weight. Channel your painful emotions with creative constructive activities you enjoy such as dancing, sports, or walking.
5. Humor—Be funny. Make yourself happy and feel better. Laughter makes difficult things easier to do.

6. Faith in God—God can help anyone to develop self-discipline. There is nothing that God cannot help us with.

7. Acceptance of suffering—It is one of the givens of life that we all have to suffer. Depriving ourselves of food we love is suffering. It is alright to live in pain. There is no gain without pain; carry your cross each day. We pay a price for everything in life.

8. Peace and Joy—Accomplishing your goal to be healthy brings you peace and joy.

9. Courage—Be free of fear. Do not be afraid to live no matter how difficult dieting to lose weight becomes.

10. Hope—Hope to be successful in accomplishing your goals, such as losing weight.

11. Work—Dieting to lower calorie intake and doing exercise is work. Do not forget your work ethic. Find role models who work hard to achieve what they want. People who are healthy work hard to stay healthy. Avoid rationalization and other less mature ego defenses. Accept reality. Being fit is not because of people's genes. Being fit is hard work.

12. Self-love and self-esteem—You will feel good when you are able to master yourself. When you follow your diet and exercise regimen, you will feel better about yourselves.

13. Understanding—Study nutrition and learn about the foods you eat. Exchange foods with similar calorie and nutritional values. The more knowledge you have about nutrition, the better your food choices becomes.

14. Play—Make your diet and exercise regimen a game, a form of play. Sometimes you lose; sometimes you win. Forgive yourself when you are unable to follow your diet. Like when you fall down, you get back up right away.

15. Happiness—Be happy with what you accomplish. Make taking care of your health a labor of love. There is true happiness in growing to be better and healthier.

16. Energy—Live without negative emotions, such as guilt, worry, anger, and envy—thoughts and emotions that pull your energy down. When you have more energy, you will accomplish your goals easier and faster. Do physical exercises every day to improve your level of energy.
17. Handle your daily stress—Handle your stress and live with the right amount of manageable stress each day.

Based on your height and weight, you can find your body mass index (BMI). The ranges for normal BMI is between 18.5 and 25; 25 to 30 is overweight, 30 to 40 is obese, and above 40 is very obese. Ask your physician during your checkup, to tell you your BMI like asking for your blood pressure. You can also calculate your own BMI by using this formula: Wt in kg divide by height in meter square

Reread the section about managing weight in chapter 7. Again, there are only two ways to lose weight:

1. Lower your calorie intake.
2. Burn more calories by doing physical exercise.

More helpful tips for dieting:

1. Know when you feel full, and stop eating after you are 80 percent full.
2. Prepare what you are going to eat ahead of time, and eat only what's on your plate.
3. Eat on schedule, and do not eat because you just feel like eating.
4. Eat what you need, not what you want.
5. To lose weight, you need to lower your calorie intake or exercise more than usual. To maintain your weight you need a stable diet and calorie expenditures.

6. Be proactive. For example, look at the food you are tempted to eat and ask yourself, "Is this healthy for me?" It takes less effort to stop yourself from eating than dieting later on to lose the weight you have gained.

To quit smoking or stop drinking, you can implement the seventeen skill sets. You can also follow the twelve-step Alcoholics Anonymous program.

To quit smoking and to stop drinking permanently are easier than dieting because you can say no to cigarettes and alcohol permanently, but obviously you cannot say no to food permanently. You will be tempted to overeat every single day. It is not unusual to lose weight and later put on weight again.

Change

I cannot change the tides
That keep touching the shores.

I cannot change the wind
That moves the persimmon trees.

But I can change
Where to look—
I look at the positive things in my life,
"I count my blessings."
What to see—
I see beauty everywhere.
I see waterlilies, camias and gardenias
In my mind's eyes.
What to do—
I do constructive activities;
I stop my unhealthy habits.

I am productive and use my life
To live and love consciously;
To change things for the better.

Discipline

We can solve our problems
With God's help.

We can solve our problems
With patience and perseverance
Like the lilies of the valley
That keeps flowering every spring;
Like the sunrise—patient and perseveres
Regardless of the weather.

We can slowly master our life
Like learning to play a musical instrument.
We can compose a life of work, love and play in one
piece.
We can accept the pain, the clouds and the rain
That come without being welcomed.

Make your life like your music.
Live the spaces between the notes
And create your own rhythm.
Dance to your own music;
Be a bird singing, a butterfly flying,
A toddler running—fearless and laughing.
Do all these with discipline.

CONCLUSION

L OSING MY BELOVED son was the most painful and biggest change in my life. Nonetheless, my greatest sorrow and suffering also brought the greatest good, as I do my best to grow from the experience. Ralph Waldo Emerson wrote the law of compensation, which says that there is always an effect for every action, or there is a cause for every effect. If you do good things, good things will follow; if you do bad things, bad things will follow. You will be rewarded by any virtues here on earth or hereafter.

Experiencing Emerson's law of compensation, I gained many things in my loss. I took the responsibility to overcome my tragedy, to become a better person—learn emotional maturity thoroughly—and become stronger because of it. From my experience, I know now, in the deepest way, that pain and suffering are really part of life, and no matter how painful life can be, we can be healed.

I want to help more people by sharing the wisdom I gained from my tragic experience. I have spent a lot of time thinking about my changing worldviews. I believe that we should always try our best to do good things and love unconditionally. We will be rewarded somehow, someday, somewhere. I have learned to live fully each day. I do not know what tomorrow will bring; tomorrow may not come at all. I have strengthened my faith and trust in God. I developed stronger empathy and compassion for people. I have more appreciation of my day-to-day life and the composition of my life. My life has had very sad and very happy occasions. I see the whole tapestry of my life as a beautiful composition—I am very grateful.

The journey through grief is not just about loss. It is also about gratitude, cherished memories, and hope. My son left me so many happy memories: the life lived together, the things we did together, his contagious and spontaneous sense of humor, sharing his brilliance—knowledge about truth and beauty, art, life, literature, music, poetry, and food. He was my walking encyclopedia. He lived what was important to him. He loved deeply and lived life to the fullest. As Seneca wrote, "Not how long it is, but how good it is, is what matters."

Hope helps me master the events of my life. I hope for better times ahead. An editorial in the *London Times* on December 14, 1984, said, "Our lives are like the course of the sun; at the darkest moment, there is a promise of daylight." Anne Frank (1929–1945) also wrote, "I don't think of all the misery, but of the beauty that still remains."

Through faith, I know that when I die, we will be together for eternity. I also have faith that Edward is joyful and at peace where he is. Whenever I talk to God, this is what I always ask God to grant me. "There is faith, hope, and love, but the greatest is love." We have loved each other deeply, and this is the most important thing.

I wrote about mature ego defenses, the journey to holiness, self-development, emotions, understanding and managing stress. These topics lead to physical and mental health, more energy, personal fulfillment, and spiritual growth. They are tributaries of one river emptying into the ocean of peace and joy (love).

We achieve peace and joy when we are emotionally mature, at the price of pain and suffering while living in this world, whereas we will have eternal life of peace and joy without pain and suffering (for those who are blessed to believe in heaven and God) after we physically die.

Resilience

We can be resilient and overcome any losses. From my personal experience, I applied the seventeen skill sets to live well whatever life brings. Again, these are: altruism (love), suppression (self-discipline), anticipation, sublimation (creativity), humor, faith in God, acceptance of suffering, peace and joy, self-love and self-esteem, courage, hope, work, understanding, play, happiness, energy, and handling stress, to help me live fully. I have accepted my tragic loss and live a peaceful and balanced life of work, love, and play. In Freudian psychoanalytic theory, ego defenses such as altruism (love), suppression (self-discipline), sublimation (creativity), anticipation, and humor are mature unconscious psychological strategies operating in one's mind to adapt to life. I have learned to use these defenses consciously by will and choice.

Our stress influences the levels of ego defenses that we use. So when we depend on our unconscious or automatic responses to adapt to life, the outcome of our behavior or defenses can be immature and destructive when we are under a lot of stress. Whereas we can master our fate, we can solve our problems consistently and constructively even when we are under severe stress when we implement these mature defenses consciously every day. No matter what life brings, even when we are under a lot of stress, we can adapt maturely when we use our will and consciously use the mature ego defenses to handle our problems.

Marietta was just laid off from her job, and the following week, she was diagnosed with stage three breast cancer. She was so angry when she came back from her doctor's appointment that she fought with her husband. Instead of doing things to improve her situation, she was even more destructive. After she thought and evaluated her situation, she consciously uses humor, altruism, suppression, sublimation, and anticipation to deal with her emotions. She ended up laughing at her unreasonable behavior (humor), she told her husband that she was sorry (altruism), she went to the gym to exercise (self-discipline), she rearranged her living room furniture (sublimation), and she spent time thinking about what she needs to do to find an oncologist (anticipation). The mature ego defenses that she chose to use consciously improved her life situation.

Resilience means the ability to accept and constructively deal with stress. It is one of the givens of this life that we go through pain and experience problems. If we do not grow, we have the same problems, which often escalate to bigger and bigger problems. Our ability to live with reasonable health, peace, joy, and fulfillment depends on our ability to grow, develop, and successfully adapt to life, to keep living maturely and continue to mold our character.

Resilience
We accept
The givens of life—
Gains, losses,
Joy, pain, sadness, suffering,
Good and bad things.

Everything is temporary—
We live, we create,
We go with the flow
Like the river moving—
Emptying into the ocean.

We make use of time,
It will never come back.
We breathe, saying to ourselves—
"Let me successfully adapt to my daily life.
This is all I have, this precious present moment."
I live fully every moment, like a beautiful butterfly—
Dancing around watching the flowers.

Adaptation to Daily Life and Living Well
Consciously change the way you think:
Unconditionally love yourself and everyone (Altruism)
Consciously delay your gratification (suppression)
Be creative is solving your problems (sublimation)
Try to foresee the consequences of what you will be doing (anticipation)
See the funny side of life (humor)

Be patient and persevere
like the tides returning to the shores.
Make the effort and the courage to grow—
be a daffodil facing the sun,
resting with the moon.

Keep growing to adapt daily
to the seasons of your life.
Physical life is short;
spiritual life is forever.

Adapt and live
in truth, goodness and beauty;
the power is within you.

Live to become unconditionally
as giving, forgiving
and compassionate to yourself
as you are to others, for the love of God;
we are all flowering buds in the same tree.

Love and live each day in the present
gratefully, happily and peacefully
with optimism and hope—
manifest the love in your soul.

Love comes from God
and ends for God.

"When you were born, you cried and the world
rejoiced. Live your life so that when you die, the world
cries and you rejoice."
—Cherokee proverb

Epilogue

M Y FIRST PASSION has always been medicine. I love my work
as an internist and primary care physician. My second
passion is learning something that will be useful for my own
personal growth and also help other people. It is important for me
to be emotionally mature, physically and mentally healthy, a good
person, and to continue to become the best person that I can be.
Writing this book not only accomplishes Edward's dream—it is
making me grow and fulfill my own.

The material in this book came from many books I have
read. As Montaigne wrote, "And one might therefore say of me
that in this book I have only made up a bunch of other people's
flowers, and that of my own I have only provided the string that
ties them together." I am like the hands in Picasso's painting,
holding a bunch of beautiful, multicolored flowers and presenting
them to others.

Glossary

Abnormal Lymphocytes

A small white blood cell (leukocyte) that plays a large role in defending the body against disease.

Lymphocytes are responsible for immune responses. There are two main types of lymphocytes: B cells and T cells. The B cells make antibodies that attack bacteria and toxins while the T cells attack body cells themselves when they have been taken over by viruses or have become cancerous. Lymphocytes secrete products (lymphokines) that modulate the functional activities of many other types of cells and are often present at sites of chronic inflammation.

Source: http://www.medterms.com/script/main/art.asp?articlekey=4220

An atypical lymphocyte is sometimes called a reactive lymphocyte. These cells are much larger than the typical lymphocyte, with a diameter that usually measures more than 30 microns. Their typical color is blue or gray, and their typical shape is round, elliptical or folded. They are generally detected during routine blood screenings.

Source: http://www.reference.com/motif/health/atypical-lymphocytes

Adrenal Cortex

The outer portion of the adrenal gland located on top of each kidney. The adrenal cortex produces steroid hormones which regulate carbohydrate and fat metabolism and mineralocorticoid hormones which regulate salt and water balance in the body.

Underfunction of the adrenal cortex results in Addison disease while overfunction occurs in the adrenogenital syndrome and in Cushing syndrome.

Source: http://www.medterms.com/script/main/art. asp?articlekey= 9704

Adrenal Gland

A small gland located on top of the kidney. The adrenal glands produce hormones that help control heart rate, blood pressure, the way the body uses food, the levels of minerals such as sodium and potassium in the blood, and other functions particularly involved in stress reactions.

Source: http://www.medterms.com/script/main/art. asp?articlekey=2154

Adrenal Medulla

The inner portion of adrenal gland. (The outer portion is the adrenal cortex).

The adrenal medulla makes epinephrine (adrenaline) and norepinephrine (noradrenaline). Epinephrine is secreted in response to low blood levels of glucose as well as exercise and stress; it causes the breakdown of the storage product glycogen to the sugar glucose in the liver, facilitates the release of fatty acids from adipose (fat) tissue, causes dilation (widening) of the small arteries within muscle and increases the output of the heart. Norepinephrine secreted by the adrenal gland acts to narrow blood vessels and raise blood pressure.

Underfunction of the adrenal medulla is virtually unknown. However, a tumor called a pheochromocytoma produces norepinephrine and epinephrine and is equivalent to overfunction of the adrenal medulla. Pheochromocytomas arise within the adrenal medulla or elsewhere in the sympathetic nervous system. They typically cause hypertension (high blood pressure) that may be paroxysmal (sharply episodic) with attacks of headaches, feelings of apprehension, sweating, flushing of the face, nausea and vomiting, palpitations and tingling of the extremities (the arms and legs).

Source: http://www.medterms.com/script/main/art. asp?articlekey= 9702

ADRENALINE

A stress hormone produced within the adrenal gland that quickens the heart beat, strengthens the force of the heart's contraction, and opens up the bronchioles in the lungs, among other effects. The secretion of adrenaline is part of the human "fight or flight" response to fear, panic, or perceived threat. It is also known as epinephrine.

Source: http://www.medterms.com/script/main/art. asp?articlekey=2155

AGAPE

Noun.

1. Love Feast
2. Love.

Source: http://www.merriam-webster.com/dictionary/agape

ALTRUISM

1. Unselfish regard for or devotion to the welfare of others.
2. Behavior by an animal that is not beneficial to or may be harmful to itself but that benefits others of its species.

Source: http://www.merriam-webster.com/dictionary/altruism

AMYGDALA

The amygdala is an almond-shaped part of the limbic system in the brain.

Source: http://www.medterms.com/script/main/art.asp?articlekey=39204

ANHEDONIA

Loss of the capacity to experience pleasure. The inability to gain pleasure from normally pleasurable experiences. Anhedonia is a core clinical feature of depression, schizophrenia, and some other mental illnesses.

An anhedonic mother finds no joy from playing with her baby. An anhedonic football fan is not excited when his team wins. An anhedonic teenager feels no pleasure from passing the driving test.

"Anhedonia" is derived from the Greek "a" (without) "hedone" (pleasure, delight). Other words derived from "hedone" include hedonism (a philosophy that emphasizes pleasure as the main aim of life), hedonist (a pleasure-seeker), and hedonophobia (an excessive and persistent fear of pleasure).

Source: http://www.medterms.com/script/main/art.asp?articlekey=17900

Applied Kinesiology

Applied kinesiology (AK) is a technique in alternative medicine used to diagnose illness or choose treatment by testing muscles for strength and weakness. Applied kinesiologists are often chiropractors, but they may also be naturopaths, medical doctors, nurses, physical therapists, veterinarians, or other health care workers. Current evidence does not support the use of applied kinesiology for diagnosis of any illness. The methodology of applied kinesiology is concerned primarily with neuromuscular function as it relates to the structural, chemical, mental, and physiologic regulatory mechanisms. According to their guidelines on allergy diagnostic testing, the American Academy of Allergy, Asthma and Immunology and the American College of Allergy, Asthma and Immunology stated there is "no evidence of diagnostic validity" of applied kinesiology.

Source: http://en.wikipedia.org/wiki/Applied_kinesiology

ASCETICISM

Asceticism (from the Greek ὄ σκησις, áskēsis, "exercise" or "training") describes a lifestyle characterized by abstinence from various worldly pleasures, often with the aim of pursuing religious and spiritual goals. Many religious traditions (e.g. Buddhism, Jainism, the Christian desert fathers) include practices that involve restraint with respect to actions of body, speech, and mind. The founders and earliest practitioners of these religions lived extremely austere lifestyles, refraining from sensual pleasures and the accumulation of material wealth. They practiced asceticism not as a rejection of the enjoyment of life, or because the practices themselves are virtuous, but as an aid in the pursuit of salvation or liberation.

Source: http://en.wikipedia.org/wiki/Asceticism

ATHEROSCLEROSIS

An arteriosclerosis characterized by atheromatous deposits in and fibrosis of the inner layer of the arteries.

Source: http://www.merriam-webster.com/medical/atherosclerosis

AUTOIMMUNE DISEASE

An illness that occurs when body tissues are attacked by the own immune system. The immune system is a complex organization within the body that is designed normally to "seek and destroy" invaders of the body, including infectious agents. Patients with autoimmune diseases frequently have unusual antibodies circulating in their blood that target their own body tissues.

Source: http://www.medterms.com/script/main/art.asp?articlekey=2402

Balikbayan Box

A balikbayan box (literally, "Repatriate box") is a ubiquitous, corrugated box containing any number of small items sent by an overseas Filipino known as a "balikbayan". Though often shipped by freight forwarders specializing in balikbayan boxes by sea, such boxes can be brought by Filipinos returning to the Philippines by air.

Source: http://en.wikipedia.org/wiki/Balikbayan_box

Source: http://www.medterms.com/script/main/art.asp?articlekey=2413

Benzodiazepines

Any of a group of aromatic lipophilic amines (as diazepam and chlordiazepoxide) used especially as tranquilizer.

Source: http://www.merriam-webster.com/dictionary/benzodiazepine

Bifurcation points

Point at which branching occurs.

Source: http://www.merriam-webster.com/dictionary/bifurcation

BIPOLAR DISORDER

Any of several mood disorders characterized usually by alternating episodes of depression and mania or by episodes of depression alternating with mild nonpsychotic excitement—called also *bipolar affective disorder, bipolar illness, manic depression, manic-depressive illness, manic-depressive psychosis*.

Source: http://www.merriam-webster.com/medical/bipolar%20disorder

BLESSED SACRAMENT

A devotional name used in the Roman Catholic Church, Eastern Catholic Churches, Old Catholic, Anglican, and Lutheran churches, to refer to the Host and Eucharistic wine after it has been consecrated in the sacrament of the Eucharist. Christians in these traditions believe in the Real Presence of Jesus Christ in the Eucharistic elements of the bread and wine.

Source: https://en.wikipedia.org/wiki/Blessed Sacrament

(BRAIN) FRONTAL LOBE

The part of each hemisphere of the brain located behind the forehead that serves to regulate and mediate the higher intellectual functions. The frontal lobes are important for controlling thoughts, reasoning, and behaviors.

Source: http://www.medterms.com/script/main/art.asp?articlekey=25285

BUDDHISM

A religion of eastern and central Asia growing out of the teaching of Gautama BUDDHA that suffering is inherent in life and that one can be liberated from it by mental and moral self-purification

Source: http://www.merriam-webster.com/dictionary

CHRONOLOGICAL PSYCHOSOCIAL STRENGTHS

Developmental psychosocial stages we need to acquire from childhood to old age.

COGNITIVE RESTRUCTURING

A psychotherapeutic process of learning to identify and dispute irrational or maladaptive thoughts, such as all-or-nothing thinking (splitting), magical thinking and emotional reasoning, which are commonly associated with many mental health disorders. Cognitive Restructuring (CR) employs many strategies, such as Socratic questioning, thought recording and guided imagery and is used in many types of therapies, including cognitive behavioral therapy (CBT), and rational emotive therapy (RET). A number of studies demonstrate considerable efficacy in using CR-based therapies.

Source: http://en.wikipedia.org/wiki/Cognitive_restructuring

COLITIS

Inflammation of the colon.

Source: http://www.merriam-webster.com/dictionary/colitis

CONSCIOUS

1. Having a mental faculties not dulled by sleep, faintness, or stupor
2. Done or acting with critical awareness

Source: http://www.merriam-webster.com/dictionary/conscious

DIABETES MELLITUS

Better known just as "diabetes"—a chronic disease associated with abnormally high levels of the sugar glucose in the blood. Diabetes is due to one of two mechanisms:

1. Inadequate production of insulin (which is made by the pancreas and lowers blood glucose) or
2. Inadequate sensitivity of cells to the action of insulin.

The two main types of diabetes correspond to these two mechanisms and are called insulin dependent (type 1) and non-insulin dependent (type 2) diabetes. In type 1 diabetes there is no insulin or not enough of it. In type 2 diabetes, there is generally enough insulin but the cells upon it should act are not normally sensitive to its action.

Source: http://www.medterms.com/script/main/art.asp?articlekey=2974

DIAZEPAM

A tranquilizer $C_{16}H_{13}ClN_2O$ used especially to relieve anxiety and tension and as a muscle relaxant.

Source: http://www.merriam-webster.com/dictionary/diazepam

Dopamine

An important neurotransmitter (messenger) in the brain.

Dopamine is classified as a catecholamine (a class of molecules that serve as neurotransmitters and hormones). It is a monoamine (a compound containing nitrogen formed from ammonia by replacement of one or more of the hydrogen atoms by hydrocarbon radicals). Dopamine is a precursor (forerunner) of adrenaline and a closely related molecule, noradrenaline. Dopamine is formed by the decarboxylation (removal of a carboxyl group) from dopa.

Source: http://www.medterms.com/script/main/art.asp?articlekey=14345

Dysthymia

A mood disorder characterized by chronic mildly depressed or irritable mood often accompanied by other symptoms (as eating and sleeping disturbances, fatigue, and poor self-esteem)—called also *dysthymic disorder.*

Source: http://www.merriam-webster.com/medical/dysthymia

Ego

The self especially as contrasted with another self or the world.

The one of the three divisions of the psyche in psychoanalytic theory that serves as the organized conscious mediator between the person and reality especially by functioning both in the perception of and adaptation to reality.

Source: http://www.merriam-webster.com/dictionary/ego

EGO DEFENSES

In Freudian psychoanalytic theory, defense mechanisms are psychological strategies brought into play by the unconscious mind to manipulate, deny, or distort reality (through processes including, but not limited to, Repression, Identification, or Rationalization), and to maintain a socially acceptable self-image or self-schema. Healthy persons normally use different defenses throughout life. An ego defense mechanism becomes pathological only when its persistent use leads to maladaptive behavior such that the physical and/or mental health of the individual is adversely affected. The purpose of ego defense mechanisms is to protect the mind/self/ego from anxiety and/or social sanctions and/or to provide a refuge from a situation with which one cannot currently cope.

Defense mechanisms are more accurately[citation needed] referred to as ego defense mechanisms, and can thus be categorized as occurring when the id impulses are in conflict with each other, when the id impulses conflict with super-ego values and beliefs, and when an external threat is posed to the ego.

Source: http://en.wikipedia.org/wiki/Defence_mechanisms

(EGO DEFENSE) SUBLIMATION

In psychology, sublimation is a mature type of defense mechanism where socially unacceptable impulses or idealizations are consciously transformed into socially acceptable actions or behavior, possibly converting the initial impulse in the long term. Freud defines sublimation as the process of deflecting sexual instincts into acts of higher social valuation, being "an especially conspicuous feature of cultural development; it is what makes it possible for higher psychical activities, scientific, artistic or ideological, to play such an important part in civilized life". Wade and Tarvis present a similar view stating that sublimation is when displacement "serves a higher cultural or socially useful purpose, as in the creation of art or inventions." Sublimation allows us to act out socially unacceptable impulses by converting them into a more acceptable form. For example, a person experiencing extreme anger might take up kick-boxing as a means of venting frustration. Freud believed that sublimation was a sign of maturity (indeed, of civilization), allowing people to function normally in culturally acceptable ways.

Source: http://en.wikipedia.org/wiki/Sublimation_(psychology)

(Ego Defense) Anticipation: to take or consider the consequences of one's behavior ahead of time.

Suppression: the ability to consciously control one's thought, desire and emotion; and express them at an appropriate time.

EMOTIONAL INTELLIGENCE

1. Emotional intelligence is the ability to identify, assess, and control the emotions of oneself, of others, and of groups. Various models and definitions have been proposed of which the ability and trait EI models are the most widely accepted in the scientific literature. Ability EI is usually measured using maximum performance tests and has stronger relationships with traditional intelligence, whereas trait EI is usually measured using self-report questionnaires and has stronger relationships with personality. Criticisms have centered on whether the construct is a real intelligence and whether it has incremental validity over IQ and the Big Five personality dimensions.

Source: http://en.wikipedia.org/wiki/Emotional_intelligence

2. Emotional intelligence (EI) refers to the ability to perceive, control and evaluate emotions. Some researchers suggest that emotional intelligence can be learned and strengthened, while others claim it is an inborn characteristic.

Source: http://psychology.about.com/od/ personalitydevelopment/a/emotionalintell.htm

EMOTIONAL MATURITY

The mature person has developed attitudes in relation to himself and his environment which have lifted him above "childishness" in thought and behavior.

Suggest: http://www.michaelppowers.com/path/mature.html

ENCULTURATION

The process by which an individual learns the traditional content of a culture and assimilates its practices and values.

Source: http://www.merriam-webster.com/dictionary/ enculturation

ENDORPHINS

A hormonal compound that is made by the body in response to pain or extreme physical exertion. Endorphins are similar in structure and effect to opiate drugs. They are responsible for the so-called runner's high, and release of these essential compounds permits humans to endure childbirth, accidents, and strenuous everyday activities.

EPINEPHRINE (Synonym *for Adrenaline*)

A substance produced by the medulla (inside) of the adrenal gland. The name epinephrine was coined in 1898 by the American pharmacologist and physiologic chemist (biochemist) John Jacob Abel who isolated it from the adrenal gland which is located above (epi-) the kidney ("nephros" in Greek). (Abel also crystallized insulin). Technically speaking, epinephrine is a sympathomimetic catecholamine. It causes quickening of the heart beat, strengthens the force of the heart's contraction, opens up the airways (bronchioles) in the lungs and has numerous other effects. The secretion of epinephrine by the adrenal is part of the fight-or-flight reaction. Adrenaline is a synonym of epinephrine and is the official name in the British Pharmacopoeia.

EROS
1. The Greek god of erotic love.
2. The sum of life-preserving instincts that are manifested as impulses to gratify basic needs, as sublimated impulses, and as impulses to protect and preserve the body and mind.
3. A: Love conceived by Plato as a fundamental creative impulse having a sensual element B: Often not capitalized: erotic love or desire.

ESCITALOPRAM OXALATE (WELLBUTRIN)

Is an antidepressant of the selective serotonin reuptake inhibitor
(SSRI) class.

Source: http://en.wikipedia.org/wiki/Escitalopram

FIBROMYALGIA

A chronic disorder characterized by widespread pain, tenderness,
and stiffness of muscles and associated connective tissue structures
that is typically accompanied by fatigue, headache, and sleep
disturbances—called also *fibromyalgia syndrome, fibromyositis.*

Source: http://www.merriam-webster.com/medical/fibromyalgia

GASTRITIS

Inflammation especially of the mucous membrane of the stomach.

Source: http://www.merriam-webster.com/dictionary/gastritis

GLUCOCORTICOID

A hormone that predominantly affects the metabolism of
carbohydrates and, to a lesser extent, fats and proteins (and has other
effects). Glucocorticoids are made in the outside portion (the cortex)
of the adrenal gland and chemically classed as steroids. Cortisol is
the major natural glucocorticoid. The term glucocorticoid also
applies to equivalent hormones synthesized in the laboratory.

Source: http://www.medterms.com/script/main/art.
asp?articlekey=3609

HYPOMANIC

Of, relating to, or affected with hypomania <depressive periods and *hypomanic* periods may be separated by periods of normal mood.

Source: http://www.merriam-webster.com/medical/hypomanic

HINDUISM

The dominant religion of India that emphasizes dharma with its resulting ritual and social observances and often mystical contemplation and ascetic practices

Source: http://www.merriam-webster.com/dictionary

INTRAPSYCHIC CONFLICTS

An emotional clash of opposing impulses within oneself, for example, of the id versus the ego or the ego versus the superego.

Source: http://medical-dictionary.thefreedictionary.com/intrapsychic+conflict

ISLAM

The religious faith of Muslims including belief in Allah as the sole deity and in Muhammad as his prophet

Source: http://www.merriam-webster.com/dictionary

LIMBIC SYSTEM

Is a set of brain structures, including the hippocampus, amygdalae, anterior thalamic nuclei, septum, limbic cortex and fornix, which seemingly support a variety of functions including emotion, behavior, motivation, long-term memory, and olfaction.

Source: http://en.wikipedia.org/wiki/Limbic_system

LORAZEPAM

An anxiolytic benzodiazepine $C_{15}H_{10}Cl_2N_2O_2$.

Source: http://www.merriam-webster.com/dictionary/lorazepam

LYMPH NODES

One of many small, bean-shaped organs located throughout the lymphatic system. The lymph nodes are important in the function of the immune response and also store special cells that can trap cancer cells or bacteria that are traveling through the body.

Source: http://www.medterms.com/script/main/art.asp?articlekey=4213

LYMPHATIC SYSTEM

Part of the circulatory system that is concerned especially with scavenging fluids and proteins that have escaped from cells and tissues and returning them to the blood, with the phagocytic removal of cellular debris and foreign material, and with immune responses, that overlaps and parallels the system of blood vessels in function and shares some constituents with it, and that consists especially of the thymus, spleen, tonsils, lymph, lymph nodes, lymphatic vessels, lymphocytes, and bone marrow where stem cells differentiate into precursors of B cells and T cells—called also *lymphoid system, lymph system.*

Source: http://www.merriam-webster.com/medical/ lymphatic%20system

1. Sexual drive.
2. In psychoanalysis, the psychic energy from all instinctive biological drives.

Libido in Latin means "desire, longing, fancy, lust, or rut." Although the adjective libidinous, meaning lustful, has been used in English for 500 or so years, libido only entered the language in 1913, thanks to Sigmund Freud and other psychoanalysts who applied the term to psychic energy or drive, and especially to the sexual instinct.

Source: http://www.medterms.com/script/main/art. asp?articlekey=4154

MANIA

Excitement of psychotic proportions manifested by mental and physical hyperactivity, disorganization of behavior, and elevation of mood; specifically: the manic phase of bipolar disorder

Source: http://www.merriam-webster.com/medical/mania

MESSIAH

1. A: The expected king and deliverer of the Jews
   B: Jesus
2. A professed or accepted leader of some hope or cause

Source: http://www.merriam-webster.com/dictionary/messiah

METABOLIC SYNDROME

A constellation of conditions that place people at high risk for coronary artery disease. These conditions include type 2 diabetes, obesity, high blood pressure, and a poor lipid profile with elevated LDL ("bad") cholesterol, low HDL ("good") cholesterol, elevated triglycerides. All of these conditions are associated with high blood insulin levels. The fundamental defect in the metabolic syndrome is insulin resistance in both adipose tissue and muscle. Drugs that decrease insulin resistance also usually lower blood pressure and improve the lipid profile.

Source: http://www.medterms.com/script/main/art.asp?articlekey=32619

MULTIPLE SCLEROSIS

A demyelinating disease marked by patches of hardened tissue in the brain or the spinal cord and associated especially with partial or complete paralysis and jerking muscle tremor.

Source: http://www.merriam-webster.com/medical/multiple%20sclerosis

Neurotransmitter

A chemical that is released from a nerve cell which thereby transmits an impulse from a nerve cell to another nerve, muscle, organ, or other tissue. A neurotransmitter is a messenger of neurologic information from one cell to another.

Source: http://www.medterms.com/script/main/art. asp?articlekey= 9973

Norepinephrine

Or noradrenaline is a catecholamine with multiple roles including as a hormone and a neurotransmitter. Areas of the body that produce or are affected by norepinephrine are described as noradrenergic.

Source: http://en.wikipedia.org/wiki/Norepinephrine

Nortriptyline

Nortriptyline is a second-generation tricyclic antidepressant (TCA) marketed as the hydrochloride salt. It is used in the treatment of major depression and childhood nocturnal enuresis (bedwetting). In addition, it is sometimes used for chronic illnesses such as chronic fatigue syndrome, chronic pain and migraine, and labile affect in some neurological conditions.

Source: http://en.wikipedia.org/wiki/Nortriptyline

The functional changes associated with or resulting from disease or injury.

Source: http://www.dictionary.reference.com/browse/pathophysiology

Source: http://en.wikipedia.org/wiki/Pareto_principle

PAROXETINE

Paroxetine (also known by the trade names Aropax, Paxil, Pexeva, Seroxat, Sereupin) is an antidepressant drug of the SSRI type. Paroxetine is used to treat major depression, obsessive-compulsive disorder, panic disorder, social anxiety, posttraumatic stress disorder and generalized anxiety disorder in adult outpatients.

Source: http://en.wikipedia.org/wiki/Paroxetine

PASALUBONG

Pasalubong is the Filipino tradition of a homecoming gift. The word is Tagalog, literally meaning "[something] meant for you when you welcome me back." It is one of the most distinctive and widely practiced Filipino traditions. Pasalubong can be any gift or souvenir brought for family, loved ones, or friends after being away for a period of time. It can also be any gift given by someone arriving from a distant place.

Source: http://en.wikipedia.org/wiki/Pasalubong

PEPTIC ULCER

An ulcer in the wall of the stomach or duodenum resulting from the digestive action of the gastric juice on the mucous membrane when the latter is rendered susceptible to its action (as from infection with the bacterium Helicobacter pylori or the chronic use of NSAIDs).

Source: http://www.merriam-webster.com/medical/peptic%20 ulcer

PERIPHERAL (AUTONOMIC NERVOUS SYSTEM)

The portion of the nervous system that is outside the brain and spinal cord. Abbreviated PNS. The nerves in the PNS connect the central nervous system (CNS) to sensory organs, such as the eye and ear, and to other organs of the body, muscles, blood vessels, and glands. The peripheral nerves include the 12 cranial nerves, the spinal nerves and roots, and the autonomic nerves. The autonomic nerves are concerned with automatic functions of the body, specifically with the regulation of the heart muscle, the tiny muscles that line the walls of blood vessels, and glands.

Source: http://www.medterms.com/script/main/art. asp?articlekey=8258

PHILIA
   1. Friendly feeling toward <Francophilia>

Source: http://www.merriam-webster.com/dictionary/philia

PHYSIOLOGICAL NEEDS

Maslow's hierarchy of needs is a theory in psychology, proposed by Abraham Maslow in his 1943 paper "A Theory of Human Motivation". Maslow subsequently extended the idea to include his observations of humans' innate curiosity. His theories parallel many other theories of human developmental psychology, all of which focus on describing the stages of growth in humans. Maslow use the terms "Physiological, Safety, Belongingness and Love, Esteem, and Self-Actualization" needs to describe the pattern that human motivations generally move through.

Source: http://en.wikipedia.org/wiki/ Maslow's hierarchy of needs

PITUITARY GLAND

The main endocrine gland. It is a small structure in the head. It is called the master gland because it produces hormones that control other glands and many body functions including growth. The pituitary consists of the anterior and posterior pituitary.

Source: http://www.medterms.com/script/main/art. asp?articlekey=4915

POST-TRAUMATIC STRESS DISORDER

A common anxiety disorder that develops after exposure to a terrifying event or ordeal in which grave physical harm occurred or was threatened. Family members of victims also can develop the disorder. PTSD can occur in people of any age, including children and adolescents. More than twice as many women as men experience PTSD following exposure to trauma. Depression, alcohol or other substance abuse, or other anxiety disorders frequently co-occur with PTSD.

Source: http://www.medterms.com/script/main/art.asp?articlekey=18779

Psychosis

In the general sense, a mental illness that markedly interferes with a person's capacity to meet life's everyday demands. In a specific sense, it refers to a thought disorder in which reality testing is grossly impaired.

Source: http://www.medterms.com/script/main/art.asp?articlekey=5110

Psycho-social Developmental Crisis

See Abnormalities in Psychosocial Stages of Development.

Psychosocial Stages of Development

Erikson's stages of psychosocial development as articulated by Erik Erikson explain eight stages through which a healthily developing human should pass from infancy to late adulthood. In each stage the person confronts, and hopefully masters, new challenges.

Each stage builds on the successful completion of earlier stages. The challenges of stages not successfully completed may be expected to reappear as problems in the future.

However, mastery of a stage is not required to advance to the next stage. Erikson's stage theory characterizes an individual advancing through the eight life stages as a function of negotiating his or her biological forces and sociocultural forces. Each stage is characterized by a psycho social crisis of these two conflicting forces (as shown in the table below). If an individual does indeed successfully reconcile these forces (favoring the first mentioned attribute in the crisis), he or she emerges from the stage with the corresponding virtue. For example, if an infant enters into the toddler stage (autonomy vs. shame & doubt) with more trust than mistrust, he or she carries the virtue of hope into the remaining life stages.

Source: http://en.wikipedia.org/wiki/
Erikson's stages of psychosocial development

PSYCHOTROPIC MEDICATIONS

Any medication capable of affecting the mind, emotions, and behavior. Some medications such as lithium, which may be used to treat depression, are psychotropic. Also called a psychodynamic medication.

Source: http://www.medterms.com/script/main/art.
asp?articlekey=30808

RATIONAL EMOTIVE THERAPY

Rational Emotive Behavior Therapy (REBT), previously called rational therapy and rational emotive therapy, is a comprehensive, active-directive, philosophically and empirically based psychotherapy which focuses on resolving emotional and behavioral problems and disturbances and enabling people to lead happier and more fulfilling lives.

Source: http://en.wikipedia.org/wiki/
Rational emotive behavior therapy

Resilience

1. The capability of a strained body to recover its size and shape after deformation caused especially by compressive stress.
2. An ability to recover from or adjust easily to misfortune or change.

Source: http://www.merriam-webster.com/dictionary/resilience

Rheumatoid Arthritis

An autoimmune disease characterized by chronic inflammation of joints. Rheumatoid disease can also involve inflammation of tissues in other areas of the body, such as the lungs, heart, and eyes. Because it can affect multiple organs of the body, rheumatoid arthritis is referred to as a systemic illness. Although rheumatoid arthritis is a chronic illness, patients may experience long periods without symptoms. Also known as rheumatoid disease.

Source: http://www.medterms.com/script/main/art. asp?articlekey=5354

Serotonin

A neurotransmitter that is involved in the transmission of nerve impulses. Serotonin can trigger the release of substances in the blood vessels of the brain that in turn cause the pain of migraine. Serotonin is also key to mood regulation; pain perception; gastrointestinal function, including perception of hunger and satiety; and other physical functions.

Source: http://www.medterms.com/script/main/art. asp?articlekey=5468

SUBCONSCIOUS

Existing in the mind but not immediately available to consciousness.

Source: http://www.merriam-webster.com/dictionary/
subconscious

SUBLIMATION

(Ego Defense) Sublimation

In psychology, sublimation is a mature type of defense mechanism where socially unacceptable impulses or idealizations are consciously transformed into socially acceptable actions or behavior, possibly converting the initial impulse in the long term. Freud defines sublimation as the process of deflecting sexual instincts into acts of higher social valuation, being "an especially conspicuous feature of cultural development; it is what makes it possible for higher psychical activities, scientific, artistic or ideological, to play such an important part in civilized life". Wade and Tarvis present a similar view stating that sublimation is when displacement "serves a higher cultural or socially useful purpose, as in the creation of art or inventions." Sublimation allows us to act out socially unacceptable impulses by converting them into a more acceptable form. For example, a person experiencing extreme anger might take up kick-boxing as a means of venting frustration. Freud believed that sublimation was a sign of maturity (indeed, of civilization), allowing people to function normally in culturally acceptable ways.

Source: http://en.wikipedia.org/wiki/Sublimation_(psychology)

SUPER-EGO

In the psychoanalytic theory of Sigmund Freud, latest developing of three agencies (with the id and ego) of the human personality. The superego is the ethical component of the personality and provides the moral standards by which the ego operates. The superego's criticisms, prohibitions, and inhibitions form a person's conscience, and its positive aspirations and ideals represent one's idealized self-image, or "ego ideal."

Source: http://www.britannica.com/EBchecked/topic/574274/superego

SYNAPSE

A place at which a nervous impulse passes from one neuron to another.

Source: http://www.merriam-webster.com/medical/synapse

TAOISM

A Chinese mystical philosophy traditionally founded by Lao-Tzu in the sixth century B.C. that teaches conformity to the Tao by unassertive action and simplicity

Source: http://www.merriam-webster.com/dictionary

TESTOSTERONE

A "male hormone"—a sex hormone produced by the testes that encourages the development of male sexual characteristics, stimulates the activity of the male secondary sex characteristics, and prevents changes in them following castration. Chemically, testosterone is 17-beta-hydroxy-4-androstene-3-one.

Source: http://www.medterms.com/script/main/art. asp?articlekey=5747

THYMUS GLAND

A glandular structure of largely lymphoid tissue that functions in cell-mediated immunity by being the site where T cells develop, that is present in the young of most vertebrates typically in the upper anterior chest or at the base of the neck, that arises from the epithelium of one or more embryonic branchial clefts, and that tends to disappear or become rudimentary in the adult.

Source: http://www.merriam-webster.com/medical/thymus

UNCONSCIOUS
   1. Not knowing or perceiving; not aware
   2. Free from self-awareness

Source: http://www.merriam-webster.com/dictionary/unconscious

UNIPOLAR DEPRESSION

A major depressive episode that occurs without the manic phase that occurs in the classic form of bipolar disorder.

Source: http://www.thefreedictionary.com/unipolar+depression

YOGA

1. A Hindu theistic philosophy teaching the suppression of all activity of body, of mind, and of will in order that the self may realize its distinction from them and attain liberation.

2. A system of exercises for attaining bodily or mental control and well-being.

Source: http://www.merriam-webster.com/dictionary/yoga

Appendix—A

H ERE ARE THE seventeen skill sets to learn and develop, to make them into a habit to successfully adapt to daily Life— to love, work, play, and be efficient in solving your day-to- day problems. Use them and make them into habits to live well whatever life brings in you.

Remember the pattern of numbers 5-3-7-1-1 for easier recall:

- Numbers one to five are our mature ego defenses, (5)
- Six, seven, and eight are part of our journey to holiness, (3)
- Nine to fifteen are part of self-development, (7)
- Sixteen is mastering emotions, thereby living with optimum energy, (1)
- Seventeen is handling life's stress (chapter 5,6,&7), (1)

Be patient. Review the seventeen skill sets often until you can easily remember and apply them as habits. Keep on applying them in your day-to-day life, Use some or all of the seventeen skill sets depending on the particular problem you need to solve at the moment.

Life is difficult. Making it a habit to use these seventeen skill sets require time, courage and work. Remember that life is not easy.

Life is complicated and there are no easy road but the seventeen skill sets you learn and develop into habits will help you live your life in the best way possible.

God bless you!

The five ego defenses are in Chapter 1

1. Love (altruism)
   The principle of living and doing things for the good of others.
   See pages 9 to 21
2. Self -discipline (suppression)
   The ability to consciously control one's thought, desire and emotion and express them at an appropriate time; or the ability to choose what to think, what to feel, and what to do at the present moment.
   See pages 21 to 24
3. Anticipation
   To take or consider the consequences of our behavior ahead of time.
   See pages 24 to 27
4. Sublimation (creativity)
   The ability to transfer aggressive and socially unacceptable biological drive for a greater social good.
   See pages 27 to 31
5. Humor
   To see the funny side of things
   See pages 31 to 35

Faith in God, Acceptance of Suffering, and Peace and Joy are in Chapter 2

6. Faith in God
   See pages 37 to 52
7. Acceptance of Suffering
   See pages 59 to 62
8. Peace and Joy
   See pages 65 to 67

Self-love and self-esteem, courage, hope. Work, understanding, play, and happiness are in Chapter 3

Energy is in Chapter 4

Handling stress and other topics on stress in Chapter 5,6,&7,

APPENDIX—B

T HE FOLLOWING ARE Catholic prayers, Judeo-Christian scriptures, The Twelve-step AA prayer, and descriptions of other Christian, Muslim, Hindu, Buddhist, and Jewish religious practices.

I.   Catholic Prayers

A. The Holy Rosary Prayers

Instructions on How to Pray the Holy Rosary

1.   Make the SIGN OF THE CROSS.
2.   Holding the Crucifix of the Rosary, recite the APOSTLES' CREED.
3.   With the first bead of the Rosary, say the LORD'S PRAYER.
4.   On each of the three beads, say the HAIL MARY for the increase of faith, hope, and charity.
5.   Say the GLORY BE.
6.   Say the first Mystery.
7.   Pray one (1) OUR FATHER.
8.   On each of the ten (10) small beads, pray the HAIL MARY.
9.   After then (10) HAIL MARY's, say the GLORY BE.
10. Recite the prayer, O MY JESUS.
11. ecall the next Mystery then repeat starting with number (7).
12. fter the reciting all the five Mysteries, pray the HAIL HOLY QUEEN and the CLOSING PRAYER.

Four mysteries of the Holy Rosary—This is the summation of the life of Jesus Christ

The Joyful Mysteries (Mondays and Saturdays)

1. The annunciation (Luke 1:28-38) Desire to do God's will
2. The visitation (Luke 1: 39-42) Humility
3. The nativity (Luke 2:1-7) Detachment from things of the world
4. The presentation (Luke 2:23-32) Obedience
5. The finding in the temple (Luke 2:45-49) Vocation

The Luminous Mysteries (Thursdays)

1. The baptism in the Jordan river (Matthew 3:16-17) Openness to the Holy Spirit
2. The manifestation at the marriage feast of cana (John 2:12) Trust in God's providence
3. The proclamation of the kingdom (Mark 1:15) Repentance
4. The transfiguration (Luke 9:28-31) Desire for Holiness
5. The institution of the Eucharist (John 6:51) Love for the Eucharist

The Sorrowful Mysteries (Tuesdays and Fridays)

1. The agony in the garden (Luke 22:41-45) Patience.
2. The scourging at the pillar (John 19:1) Self-control
3. The crowning with thorns (Matthew 27:27-30) Moral courage
4. The carrying of the cross (John 19:17-18) The desire to lay down our lives for others
5. The crucifixion (Luke 23:42-46) Surrender

The Glorious Mysteries (Wednesdays and Sundays)

1. The resurrection (Mark 16-17) Faith
2. The ascension (Mark 16:15-20) Hope
3. The descent of the Holy Spirit (Acts 2:1-4) Wisdom
4. The assumption (Revelation 12:1, 12:7) Purity
5. The coronation (Song of Songs 4:7-12) Friendship with Mary

1. The Sign of the Cross
   In the name of the Father,
   and of the Son,
   and of the Holy Spirit. Amen

2. The Apostles' Creed
   I believe in God,
   the Father Almighty,
   creator of heaven and earth,
   and in Jesus Christ, his only son, Our Lord,
   Who was conceived by the Holy Spirit,
   born of the Virgin Mary,
   suffered under Pontius Pilate,
   was crucified, died and was buried;
   He descended into hell;
   On the third day He rose again from the dead;
   He ascended into heaven,
   and is seated into the right hand
   of God the father almighty;
   from there he will come to judge
   the living and the dead.
   I believe in the Holy Spirit,
   the holy Catholic Church,
   the communion of saints,
   the forgiveness of sins,
   the resurrection of the body,
   And life everlasting.
   Amen.

3. The Lord's Prayer. Feel the prayer in your heart and soul.
   Our Father who are in Heaven
   Hallowed be thy name
   Thy kingdom come
   Thy will be done on earth as it is in Heaven
   Give us this day
   Our daily bread

Forgive us our trespasses
As we forgive those
Who trespass against us
And lead us not into temptation
But deliver us from evil.
Amen.
(Matthew 6:9)

4. Hail Mary
   Hail Mary, full of Grace, the Lord is with thee, blessed art
   thou amongst women and blessed is the fruit of thy womb
   Jesus. Holy Mary, Mother of God, pray for us sinners now
   and at the hour of our death. Amen.
   (Luke 1:28)

5. Glory Be
   Glory be to the Father, to the Son, and to the Holy Spirit;
   As it was in the beginning, is now, and ever shall be world
   without end. Amen

6. O My Jesus
   O my Jesus, forgive us our sins,
   save us from the fires of hell,
   and bring all souls to heaven,
   especially those who need
   most of your mercy.

7. Hail Holy Queen
   Hail, Holy Queen, Mother of Mercy!
   Hail, our life, our sweetness,
   and our hope!
   To you do we cry,
   poor banished children of eve;
   to you do we send up our sighs,

mourning and weeping
in this valley of tears.

Turn then, most gracious advocate,
your eyes of mercy towards us;
and after this our exile,
show unto us
the blessed fruit of your womb Jesus,
O clement, O loving,
O sweet Virgin Mary.
Amen.

8. The Closing Prayer
   Pray for us, O holy Mother of God.
   That we may be made worthy of the
   promises of Christ.

B. Prayers of St. Francis of Assisi (1182-1226)
   Lord, make me an instrument of your Peace.
   Where there is hatred, let me sow love;
   Where there is injury, pardon;
   Where there is doubt, faith;
   Where there is despair, hope;
   Where there is darkness, light;
   And where there is sadness, joy.

   O Divine Master, grant that I may not so much seek
   To be consoled as to console;
   To be understood as to understand;
   To be loved as to love;
   For it is in giving that we receive,
   It is in pardoning that we are pardoned;
   And it is in dying that we are born to eternal light

C. Meditate on the Fourteen Stations of the Cross:
1. Jesus is Condemned to Die.
2. Jesus is Made to Bear His Cross.
3. Jesus Falls the First Time.
4. Jesus Meets His Mother.
5. Simon Helps Jesus Carry His Cross.
6. Veronica Wipes Jesus' Face.
7. Jesus Falls the Second Time.
8. Jesus Meets the Women of Jerusalem.
9. Jesus Falls the Third Time.
10. Jesus is Stripped.
11. Jesus is Nailed to the Cross.
12. Jesus Dies on the Cross.
13. Jesus is Taken Down from the Cross.
14. Jesus is Laid in the Tomb.

In the Catholic teachings: the Holy Mass, saying the Holy Rosary, wearing the miraculous medal scapular and meditating on the Fourteen Stations of the Cross are the gateways to Heaven. The Holy Mass is centered on the Holy Eucharist, where the bread and wine are transformed into the body and blood of Jesus Christ.

II. Judeo-Christian Scriptures

The Ten Commandments

1. I am the Lord your God. You shall not have strange gods before me.
2. You shall not take the name of the Lord your God in vain.
3. Remember to keep holy the Sabbath day.
4. Honor your father and mother.
5. You shall not kill.
6. You shall not commit adultery.
7. You shall not steal.

8. You shall not bear false witness against your neighbor.
9. You shall not covet your neighbor's wife.
10. You shall not covet your neighbor's goods.

Isaiah

Isaiah 40:28–31 (780)

Do you not know
or have you not 'heard?
The Lord is the eternal God,
creator of the ends of the earth.
He does not faint nor grow weary,
and his knowledge is beyond scrutiny.
He gives strength to the fainting;
for the weak he makes vigor abound.
Though young men faint and grow weary,
and youths stagger and fall,
They that hope in the Lord will renew their strength,
They will soar as with eagles' wings;
They will run and not grow weary,
Walk and not grow faint.

Isaiah 41:10 (780)

Fear not, I am with you;
be not dismayed; I am your God.
I will strengthen you, and help you,
and uphold you with my right hand of
justice.

Psalm 23

The Lord is my shepherd;
there is nothing I lack.

In green pastures you let me graze;
to safe waters you lead me;
You restore my strength.
You guide me along the right path
for the sake of Your name.
Even when I walk through a dark valley,
I fear no harm for You are at my side;
Your rod and staff give me courage.
You set a table before me
as my enemies watch;
You anoint my head with oil;
my cup overflows.
Only goodness and love will pursue me
all the days of my life;
I will dwell in the house of the Lord
for years to come.

III. The Alcoholics Anonymous Prayer
Memorize and apply the *Twelve-step AA prayer*. There are 300 *offshoot* programs such as Al-anon, Overeaters anonymous, etc. derived from the AA program. If you have some form of addiction or destructive cravings and habits that are making your life dysfunctional, commit to joining one of the anonymous meetings.

We:

1. Admitted we were powerless over alcohol—that our lives had become unmanageable.
2. Came to believe that a Power greater than ourselves could restore us to sanity.
3. Made a decision to turn our will and our lives over to the care of God as we understood Him.
4. Made a searching and fearless moral inventory of ourselves.

5. Admitted to God, to ourselves, and to another human being the exact nature of our wrongs.
6. Were entirely ready to have God remove all these defects of character
7. Humbly asked Him to remove our shortcomings.
8. Made a list of all persons we had harmed, and became willing to make amends to them all.
9. Made direct amends to such people wherever possible, except when to do so would injure them or others.
10. Continued to take personal inventory, and when we were wrong, promptly admitted it.
11. Sought through prayer and meditation to improve our conscious contact with God as we understood Him, praying only for knowledge of His will for us and the power to carry that out.
12. Having had a spiritual awakening as the result of these steps, we tried to carry this message to alcoholics, and to practice these principles in all our affairs.

—Bill Wilson, founder of the AA program

Spiritual growth is a lifetime endeavor. The more we read, pray, and meditate on spiritual things, the more we grow spiritually. The closer we are to God, the better our life becomes.

Whatever religion you practice or find interesting, keep studying. If you are not spiritual now, start right away. It is never too late to develop your spirituality. If you are an atheist or an agnostic, be open to any religious and spiritual literature. They are food for your soul.

Faith is a gift from God. Faith fluctuates and grows over time. Do meditation and contemplation regularly. Learn to pray. There are so many ways of praying. Develop your own ways of communing with God.

CHRISTIANITY

Christians who are not Catholic believe in Jesus Christ, but do not acknowledge and pray to the Blessed Virgin mother and the Catholic saints. They talk directly to God and ask for forgiveness instead of confessing to priests for their sins as Catholics do.

Many small Christian religious denominations do not believe in the Holy Trinity. Some do not believe Jesus Christ to be the Son of God. Among them are: Scientologists, Mormons (Latter Day Saints), the Unification Church, Oneness Pentecostals, Christadelphians, the Worldwide Church of God, and Christian Scientists.

JUDAISM

Followers of Judaism believe in the Old Testament, transmitted from God to Israel through Moses and other authors. Jews mainly study the Torah which consists of the Pentateuch, the first five books of the Bible (Genesis, Exodus, Leviticus, Numbers, and Deuteronomy.) It is an inspiration and instruction on how to live. The core of the Old Testament's ethical heritage is righteousness and love of neighbor.

The New Testament was written by the followers of Jesus Christ, recounting his life after he died and was resurrected. Jesus and his disciples were Jews. According to Christian beliefs, the New Testament is a continuation of the Old Testament. For those of the Jewish faith, what some Christians refer to as Old Testament is complete in itself. For Christians, there is the belief that Jesus was the fulfillment of promises made to Israel in the Old Testament.

Prayer is an integral part of Jewish life. They have special prayers for men and another set of prayers for women. Prayers are usually recited in Hebrew, the language of Jewish thought. To Jews, the most important thing in praying is to practice introspection, seeing their role in the universe and their relationship to God.

Praying increases their awareness of God in their lives and the role that God plays in their lives.

There are orthodox, conservative, and reform forms of Judaism. They have many prayers—prayers for as soon as they wake up, before performing their mitzvah (commandment), grace after meals, whenever good or bad things happen—all these in addition to formal prayer services, which are performed three times per day every weekday and an additional time on Shabbat and during festivities. They have group prayers. A quorum of ten people is called *minyan*.

ISLAM

Muslims acknowledge Jesus as a prophet but do not believe that Jesus Christ is the son of God; they do not also believe in Jesus' crucifixion and resurrection. Muslims believe that there is no God but Allah, and Mohammad is his prophet.

Muslim religious practice:

There are five pillars of Islam; these are:

1. Fasting during the month of Ramadan,
2. giving 2.5 percent of income to charity,
3. Going on a pilgrimage to Mecca at least once a year for those who can afford.
4. Worshiping their God, Allah; ask Him for forgiveness and mercy.
5. Facing the direction of the Kabah five times per day when offering their prayers.

Prayers are very important in the practice of Islam. It is fundamental to perform the prayer correctly. It is believed that communication with Allah will bring to the prayerful people's lives courage. They pray five times a day based on the time of the falling and rising of the sun. So, the times vary depending on the seasons. They prepare their body, clothes they wear, follow rules on how men and women cover their bodies, and clean their surroundings. They have many prayers and read the Quran when they pray.

Christians and Muslims have things in common:

1. They want fairness and compassion toward the sick and needy,
2. They strive to do good but know that they are imperfect,
3. They face death, sometimes sadness, loneliness, disappointment and troubles,
4. They want to know the meaning of life and love,
5. They seek God as the answer to their problems and their questions.

HINDUISM

Hindus' law of life is love. "All love is expansion, all selfishness is contraction." Hindus believe in karma and reincarnation. They believe in one God (Brahma) but worship many gods. Krishna is one of the popular gods. They practice meditation, ask God and gods for mercy and forgiveness, and offer thanksgiving. Prayers and worship (paja) are an integral part of the Hindu religion. Yoga and meditation are also considered as a form of devotional service to the Lord. The chanting of mantras is the most popular form of worship, done at a family shrine or at the temple. They use *maalaas*, Hindu praying beads for their repetitive prayers. Here is a sample mantra: "Let all be happy. Let all be free from disease. Let all see the truth. May no one experience suffering." Meditation stills the mind in order to focus on God. Yoga is a form of meditation to tap our soul.

Buddhists believe in reincarnation and preach their four noble truths. These are:

Life is suffering.
Our attachments are the cause of our suffering.
Getting rid of our attachments gets rid of our suffering.

There are eightfold paths to the end of our suffering:

- right understanding,
- right thought,
- right speech,
- right action,
- right livelihood,
- right effort,
- right mindfulness, and
- right concentration.

Without the capacity for mental concentration and insight, Buddhists explain that one's mind is left undeveloped and unable to grasp the true nature of things. Vices, such as greed, anger, hatred, and envy are derived from this ignorance. Compassion is practiced in Buddhism as a way of life, as a way of accepting human ignorance.

Devotional meditation and the practice of loving kindness are the essence of Buddhism. Buddhists do not pray directly to a creator, God, or to Buddha. They meditate to practice loving kindness for themselves and for the world. Buddhists use beads for concentration when meditating. The prayer beads are a traditional tool used to count the number of times a mantra is recited while meditating.

When they send the loving kindness prayer, they visualize the person they are sending to as well, happy, and peaceful also. They practice compassion, and, like practitioners of the Hindu religion, believe in reincarnation.

There are many different forms of Buddhism worldwide. They have different ways of chanting and meditating, organized by various leaders. Their highest level of spiritual development is enlightenment, the same spiritual level reached by Jesus Christ, Buddha, and Krishna, as tested by Dr. David Hawkins in his research on the levels of consciousness.

Appendix — C

Excerpts from "The New American Bible"

R EMEMBER AND APPLY *St. Paul's Letter to the Corinthians on love.*
Love is patient and kind;
Love is not jealous or boastful;
It is not arrogant or rude.
Love does not insist
on its own way;
it is nor irritable or resentful;
but rejoices in the right.
Love bears all things,
hopes all things,
endures all things.
Love never ends....
1 Corinthians 13:4-8

We demonstrate our love for God by loving ourselves and people unconditionally. Practice empathy and compassion. Rise above your pride and prejudice. Remember to be humble and do not prejudge other people based on their outward appearances, power, social status or socio-economic level.

Acts

Acts 1:8 (1170–1171)

Luke said, "But you will receive power when the Holy Spirit comes upon you, and you will be my witnesses in Jerusalem, throughout Judea and Samaria, and to the ends of the earth."

Colossians 3:12-13

Put on then, as God's chosen ones, holy
and beloved, heartfelt compassion, kindness,
humility, gentleness, and patience, bearing
with one another and forgiving one another, if
one has grievance against another; as the Lord
has forgiven you, so must you also do.

John

John 3:16 (1141)

For God so loved the world that He gave His only Son, so that everyone who believes in Him might not perish but might have eternal life.

John 8:12 (1149)

Jesus spoke to them again, saying, "I am the light of the world. Whoever follows me will not walk in darkness, but will have the light of life."

John 10:10

Jesus said, "A thief comes only to steal and slaughter and destroy; I came so that they might have life and have it more abundantly."

Luke

Luke 9:23 (1109)

Then He said to all, "If anyone wishes to come after me, he must deny himself and take up his cross daily and follow me."

Luke 17:23

Jesus said, "The kingdom of Heaven is among you."

Luke 18:27

And he said, "What is impossible for human beings is possible for God."

Luke 11:13

Jesus said, "If you then, who are wicked, know how to give good gifts to your children, how much more will the Father in heaven give the Holy Spirit to those who ask Him?"

Mark

Mark 9:23 (1078)

Jesus said to him, "'If you can!' Everything is possible to one who has faith."

Matthew

Matthew 17:20 (1037)

He said to them, "Because of your little faith. Amen, I say to you, if you have faith the size of a mustard seed, you will say to this mountain, 'Move from here to there,' and it will move. Nothing will be impossible for you."

Matthew 9:29 (1022)

Then He touched their eyes and said, "Let it be done for you according to your faith."

Matthew 25:40 (1054)

And the king will say to them in reply, 'Amen, I say to you, whatever you did for one of these least brothers of mine, you did for me.'

Philippians

Philippians 4:13 (1291)

I [Paul] have the strength for everything through him who empowers me.

Philippians 1:21 (1287)

For to me life is Christ, and death is gain.

Philippians 4:8

Finally, brethren, whatever is true, whatever is right, whatever is pure, whatever is lovely, whatever is of good refute, if there is any excellence and if there is anything worthy of praise, let your mind dwell on these things.

Psalms

Psalm 37:5

Commit everything you do to the Lord
Trust Him, and He will help you.

Psalm 63

O God, You are my God–
    for You I long!
For You my body yearns;
    for You my soul thirsts,
Like a land parched, lifeless,
    and without water.
So I look to You in the sanctuary
    to see Your power and glory.
For Your love is better than life;
    my lips offer You worship!

Psalm 103

Bless the Lord, my soul;
all my being, bless his holy name!
Bless the Lord, my soul;
do not forget all the gifts of God,
Who pardons all our sins,
heals all your life.
Delivers your life from the pit,
surrounds you with love and compassion,
Fills your days with good things,
your youth is renewed like the eagle's.

Proverbs

Proverb 3:5-6

Trust in the Lord with all your heart,
on your own intelligence rely not;
In all the ways be mindful of Him,
and He will make straight thy paths.

Romans

Romans 3:23 (1213)

Paul said, "All have sinned and are deprived of the glory of God."

Romans 6:23 (1217)

Paul said, "For the wages of sin is death, but the gift of God is
eternal life in Christ Jesus our Lord."

APPENDIX D

Quotations and Poems

Mother Teresa's Teaching

The fruit of Silence is Prayer
The fruit of Prayer is Faith
The fruit of Faith is Love
The fruit of Love is Service
The fruit of Service is Peace

Apache Blessing
May the sun
bring you new energy by day,
May the moon
softly restore you by night
May the rain wash away your worries,
May the breeze
blow new strength into your being,
May you walk
gently through the world and know
its beauty all the days of your life

Mahatma Karamachard Gandhi

Seven Deadly Sins

Wealth without work
Pleasure without conscience
Science without humanity
Knowledge without character
Politics without principle
Commerce without morality
Worship without sacrifice

Rudyard Kipling

If

If you can keep your head when all about you
Are losing theirs and blaming it on you,
If you can trust yourself when all men doubt you,
But make allowance for their doubting too;
If you can wait and not be tired by waiting,
Or being lied about, don't deal in lies,
Or being heated, don't give way to hating,
And yet don't look too good, nor talk too wise:

If you can dream–and not make dreams your master,
If you can think–and not make thoughts your aim;
If you can meet with Triumph and Disaster
And treat those two impostors just the same;
If you can bear to hear the truth you've spoken
Twisted by knaves to make a trap for fools,
Or watch the things you gave your life to, broken,
And stop and build 'em up with worn–out tools:

If you can make one heap of all your winnings
And risk it all on one turn of pitch-and-toss,
And lose, and start again at your beginnings
And never breathe a word about your loss;
If you can force your heart and nerve and sinew
To serve your turn long after they are gone,
And so hold on when there is nothing in you
Except the will which says to them: "Hold on!"

If you can talk with crowds and keep your virtue,
Or walk with kings–nor lose the common touch,
If neither foes nor loving friends can hurt you,
If all men count with you, but none too much;
If you can fill the unforgiving minutes
With sixty seconds' worth of distance run,
Yours is the Earth and everything that's in it,
And–which is more–you'll be a Man, my son!

Ralph Waldo Emerson

Success

To laugh often and love much
To win the respect of intelligent persons and the affection of
children,
To earn the appreciation of honest critics
To endure the betrayal of false friends
To appreciate beauty
To find the best in others
To leave this world a little bit better whether by a healthy
Child, a garden patch, or a redeemed social condition
To know even one life breathed easier because you have
Lived—this is to have succeeded.

Pierre Teilhard de Chardin, S.J.

Someday, after we have mastered
the winds, the waves, the tide
and gravity, we shall harness for God
the energies of love.
Then, for the second time in the history
of the world, man will have discovered fire.

BIBLIOGRAPHY

INTRODUCTION

Binstock, Louis. *The Power of Maturity*. New York, NY: Hawthorn Books, Inc., 1969.

CHAPTER 1

Fromm, Erich. *The Art of Loving*. New York, NY: Harper & Row, 1985.

Hartdergen, Stephen J. *The New American Bible*. Iowa Falls, IA: World Bible Publishers, Inc., 1987.

May, Rollo. *The Courage to Create*. New York, NY: W.W. Norton & Company, Inc., 1969.

May, Rollo. *Love and Will*. New York, NY: W.W. Norton & Company, Inc., 1975.

Silverman, Kenneth. *Benjamin Franklin: The Autobiography and Other Writings*. New York, NY: Penguin Classics, 1986.

Vaillant, George E. *The Wisdom of the Ego*. Cambridge, MA: Harvard University Press, 1993.

Vaillant, George E. *Adaptation to Life,* Little, Brown & Co., 1977

CHAPTER 2

Brady, Ignatius O.F.M. *The Writings of Saint Francis of Assisi*. Assisi, Italy: Edizioni Porziuncola, 1983.

Daughters of St. Paul. *The Bible for Young Readers*. Boston, MA: The Daughters of St. Paul.

Esoteric Taijitu Yin Yang - Image Page." *Esoteric Taijitu Yin Yang*. N.p., 2009. Web. 25 Jan. 2013.

<http://guides.wikinut.com/img/43ohfxqhvpatyg61/ Esoteric-Taijitu-Yin-Yang>.

Halberstam, Yitta and Leventhal, Judith. *Small Miracles: Extraordinary Coincidences from Everyday Life.* Holbrook, Massachusetts: Adams Media Corporation, 1997.

Javary, Cyrille. *Understanding the I Ching.* Boston, MA., London, Shambala, 1997.

Jovanovic, Maha M. "Yin Yang Original." *Yin Yang Original.* N.p., n.d. Web. 25 Jan. 2013. <http://www.sensiart.com/ Pages/Spiritual/YinYang/Yin Yang Original.html>.

Kubler-Ross, Elisabeth, M.D. *On Death and Dying: What the Dying Have to Teach Doctors, Nurses, Clergy, and Their Own Families.* New York, NY: Touchstone Book, 1969.

Lewis, C.S. *Surprised by Joy.* San Diego, CA: Harvest/ HBJ Book: Harcourt Brace Jovanovich, Publishers, 1984.

Mitchell, Stephen. *Tao Te Ching.* New York, NY: Haper Collins Publisher, 1988.

Mottola, Anthony, Ph.D. *The Spiritual Exercises of St. Ignatius.* New York, NY: Doubleday, 1964.

Murphy, Joseph. *The Amazing Laws of Cosmic Mind Power.* West Nyack, NY: Parker Publishing Company, Inc., 1965.

Piper, Don with Murphey, Cecil. *90 Minutes in Heaven.* Grand Rapids, MI: Fleming H. Revell, 2004.

Walpola, Rahula, and Paul Demieville. *What the Buddha Taught.* New York: Grove, 1974.

CHAPTER 3

Becker, Dr. Irving and Ellis, Dr. Albert. *A Guide to Personal Happiness.* No. Hollywood, CA: Melvin Powers Wilshire Book Company, 1982.

Borys, Peter N. Jr. *Transforming Heart and Mind: Learning from the Mystics.* Mahwah, NJ: Paulist Press, 2006.

Chopra, Deepak. *The Seven Spiritual Laws of Success: A Practical Guide to the Fulfillment of Your Dreams.* San Rafael, CA: Amber Allen Publishing and New World Library, 1994.

Covey, Stephen R. *The 7 Habits of Highly Effective People.* New York, NY: Fireside Book, 1989.

Elkins, Dr. Dov Peretz. *Self Concept Sourcebook: Ideas & Activities for Building Self-esteem.* Rochester, NY: Growth Associates, 1979.

Erikson, Erik H. *Identity and the Life Cycle.* New York, NY: W.W. Norton & Company, Inc., 1980.

Erikson, Erik H. *The Life Cycle Completed.* New York, NY: W.W. Norton & Company, Inc., 1982.

Hocke, Robert H. *There are No Accidents: Synchronicity and the Stories of Our Lives.* New York, NY: Riverhead Books, 1997.

Johnson, Spencer, M.D. *One Minute for Myself: How to Manage Your Most Valuable Asset.* New York, NY: Avon Books, 1985

Power–Waters, Alma. *Mother Seton and the Sisters of Charity.* San Francisco, CA: Ignatius Press, 1985.

CHAPTER 4

Coles, Robert. *The Moral Life of Children.* Boston, MA: Houghton Mifflin Company, 1986.

Goleman, Daniel. *Emotional Intelligence.* New York, NY: Bantam Books, 1995.

Hawkins, David R., M.D., Ph.D. *Power vs. Force: The Hidden Determinants fo Human Behavior.* Carlsbad, CA: Hay House, Inc. 2002.

Malone, Thomas Patrick, M.D., Patrick Thomas Malone, M.D. *The Art of Intimacy.* New York, NY: Prentice Hall Press, 1987.

Peale, Norman Vincent. *The Amazing Result of Positive. Thinking,* NJ: Prentice Hall, 1959

Warren, Rick. *The Purpose Driven Life: What on Earth am I Here For?* Grand Rapids, MI: Zondervan, 2002.

Whitfield, Charles L, M.D. *A Gift to Myself.* Deerfield Beach, FL: Health Communications, Inc., 1990.

CHAPTER 5

Bernardin, Joseph. The Gift of Peace: Personal Reflections. Chicago: Loyola, 1997. Print.

CHAPTER 6

Abraham, Jeremiah. *Reclaiming the Inner Child.* Los Angeles, CA: J.P. Tarcher, 1990.

Autonomic Nervous System. *Autonomic Nervous System.* University of Minnesota, n.d.Web.25Jan2013.<http://facultypages.morris.umn.edu/~ratliffj/images/brain slides/autonomic ns1.htm>.

Boeree, George C. "The Limbic System." *The Limbic System.* N.p., 2009. Web. 08 Feb. 2013. <http://webspace.ship.edu/cgboer/limbicsystem.html>.

Jung, Carl. *The Undiscovered Self.* Boston, New York: Little, Brown, 1957.)

Levinson, Harold N., M.D. with Carter, Steven. *Phobia Free: A Medical Breakthrough Linking 90% of all Phobias and Panic Attacks to a Hidden Physical Problem.* New York, NY: M. Evans and Company, Inc., 1986.

Organization of the Nervous System. *The Peripheral Nervous System.* N.p., 2 Mar. 2011. Web. 25 Jan. 2013. <http://users.rcn.com/jkimball.ma.ultranet/BiologyPages/P/PNS.html>.

Porter, Robert S. and Justin L. Kaplan. *The Merck Manual of Diagnosis and Therapy.* Whitehouse Station, NJ: Merck Sharp &Dohme, 2011.

Santos, Deon, Tyler Pina, and Mylia Crabb. "Lymphatic System." *Lymphatic-system.* N.p., n.d. Web. 25 Jan. 2013. <http://lymphatic-system.wikispaces.com/>.

Vina, Mariela. "Los Super Neurotransmisores Del Cerebro." *suplementosnutricionales.com.uy RSS.* Capsulas De Salud, 25 May 2010. Web. 25 Jan. 2013.

Wiener, Charles M, et al. *Harrison's Principles of Internal Medicine: Self-assessment and Board Review.* New York: McGraw-Hill, Medical Pub. Division, 2008.

CHAPTER 7

Benson, Herbert, M.D. *The Relaxation Response.* New York, NY: William Morrow and Company, Inc., 1975.

Carlson, Richard, Ph.D. and Kristine. *Don't Sweat The Small Stuff in Love: Simple Ways to Nurture and Strengthen Your Relationships While Avoiding the Habits That Break Down Your Loving Connection.* New York, NY: Hyperion, 1999.

Childre, Doc and Rozman, Deborah, Ph.D. *Transforming Stress: The HeartMath® Solution for Relieving Worry, Fatigue, and Tension.* Oakland, CA: New Harbinger Publications, Inc., 2005.

Ellis, Albert, Ph.D. *How to Stubbornly Refuse to Make Yourself Miserable About Anything – Yes Anything!* New York, NY: Carol Publishing Group, 1988.

Kleiner, Susan, Ph.D., R.D., with Condor, Bob. *The Good Mood Diet: Feel Great While You Lose Weight.* New York, NY: Springboard Press, 2007.

Selye, Hans, M.D. *Stress Without Distress: How to Use Stress as a Positive Force to Achieve a Rewarding Life Style.* New York, NY: New American Library, 1974.

Wright, Eileen, M.D. "Neurotransmitters Play a New Role in Health." *Neurotransmitters Play a New Role in Health.* Ashland Citizen - Times, 12 Sept. 2003. Web. 25 Jan. 2013. <http://www.anapsid.org/cnd/hormones/neurotransmitters.html>.

CHAPTER 8

Hill, Napoleon *"You Can Work Your Own Miracles"* A Faucet Gold Medal Book, Published by Ballantine Books, 1971.

M. Scott Peck, M.D. *The Road Less Traveled.* New York, NY: Simon and Schuster, 2002

Jahoda, Marie *Wikipedia.* 12 May 2012. Web. 04 Jan. 2013. <http://en.wikipedia.org/wiki/Marie   Jahoda>.

CONCLUSION

Flach, Frederic, M.D. *Resilience: Discovering a New Strength at Times of Stress.* New York: Ballantine Books, 1988.

APPENDIX—B

The Ten Commandments. *Catechism of the Catholic Church.* Saint Charles Borromeo Publishers, 2012. Web. 26 Dec. 2012. <http://www.vatican.va/archive/ccc css/archive/catechism/command.htm>.

ABOUT THE AUTHOR

T HROUGH THE YEARS, while practicing as a Board Certified Internist in Elizabeth, NJ, Dr. Pilar Tan has dedicated herself to the wellness of her patients. She raised two beautiful and talented children, both of whom pursued professional careers. Her daughter, Melin, an accomplished pianist, chose medicine as her life's career, while her son, Edward, pursued the law and writing as his life's work.

Pilar has always been a spiritual person learning as much from her patients as she has been able to impart to them. As she continued to tend to her practice and raise her children, Pilar also began writing. Pilar wrote and published her first book, *Learning and Being*, a collection of poems and life lessons written to help and inspire her patients.

After the untimely death of her son Edward, Pilar searched for ways to overcome grief and move forward. With the help of faith, family, and friends, Pilar was able to hope for better times and begin healing. Through this process, a desire was kindled within her, to use her own personally horrific experience to help others love and live well.